1939-40 Debate Squad

THE NEW WESTERN FRONT

Books by Stuart Chase

THE TRAGEDY OF WASTE

MEN AND MACHINES

PROSPERITY: FACT OR MYTH

THE NEMESIS OF AMERICAN BUSINESS

MEXICO

A NEW DEAL

THE ECONOMY OF ABUNDANCE

GOVERNMENT IN BUSINESS

RICH LAND, POOR LAND

THE TYRANNY OF WORDS

YOUR MONEY'S WORTH
(*With F. J. Schlink*)

THE NEW WESTERN FRONT

The New Western Front

BY STUART CHASE

IN COLLABORATION WITH

MARIAN TYLER

New and Revised Edition

Harcourt, Brace and Company

New York

Typography by Robert Josephy

PRINTED IN THE UNITED STATES OF AMERICA

I HAVE ever deemed it fundamental for the United States never to take an active part in the quarrels of Europe. Their political interests are entirely distinct from ours. Their mutual jealousies, their balance of power, their complicated alliances, their forms and principles of government, are all foreign to us. They are nations of eternal war. . . . On our part, never had a people so favorable a chance of trying the opposite system, of peace and fraternity with mankind, and the direction of all our means and faculties to the purpose of improvement instead of destruction.

THOMAS JEFFERSON, 1823

CONTENTS

THE NEW WESTERN FRONT

1. A STRANGE MAP

SUPPOSE the United States were like Europe—like Europe in peacetime, to make the picture simpler as well as brighter.

I am a citizen, let us say, of *Atlantica*, a small nation without coal or iron deposits, in the northeast corner. A navy is being rushed to completion at Boston, and a fleet of bombing planes at Springfield. To the west and south of *Atlantica* lies your nation of *Hudsonia*. It has just increased its standing army by 150,000. New York, Albany, Buffalo, Pittsburgh, have complete anti-aircraft defense systems and blackout drills. We are historic enemies, you and I, pledged to each other's destruction.

Long Island used to belong to *Atlantica*. In the last great war, *Hudsonia* annexed it, and my country has nursed a spirit of revenge ever since. When we look across the Sound and see the white dunes of Long Island, we clench our fists. Our people over there, ground under the brutal heel of an oppressor. We will rescue them, if it takes our last brave soldier.

Look at the twenty hypothetical countries on the accompanying map. Every one of them has a big army and a massive tariff wall. Between the great powers of *Hudsonia* and *Huron* there is a "Maginot Line" of steel and concrete forts, running from Lake Erie to the Ohio. It is said to have cost three billion dollars. My country has an alliance with *Huron*, but *Hudsonia* doesn't know it. It is a secret treaty. We will attack from both sides when Der Tag comes. We will crucify those Dutchmen.

The standing armies of the twenty nations total almost four million men. In addition, sixteen million trained reservists are ready to spring to the colors, twenty sets of colors, remember. The total budget for armaments is twelve billion dollars a year. It takes, however, several hours of calculation to translate the various currencies into dollars. The *spondulik* of *Yellowstone*, with its three different values, is especially hard to calculate.

Every nation bordering on the coast has a navy. *Hudsonia* has ten battleships and *Sierra* has twelve. Can *Hudsonia* tolerate this inferiority? It cannot. Three super-dreadnoughts have been laid down, at $60,000,000 each. The Yonkers navy yard is blazing with activity. The six nations which have no access to the sea or to the Great Lakes are very unhappy. Their sovereign rights are threatened by hostile neighbors. They plot and threaten and scheme to win a seaport.

The free city of Baltimore is a traditional bone of contention between *Piedmont* (capital, Richmond) and *Hudsonia*. *Appalachia* also casts an imperial eye on Baltimore. Citizens of that distressed city can hardly sleep for the rival bands, bombs and parades of the orange shirts, lemon shirts and prune shirts of the three rival powers.

Observe poor *Bluegrass*, cut in two by the "Mississippi Corridor," which now belongs to *Delta*. *Delta* and *De-*

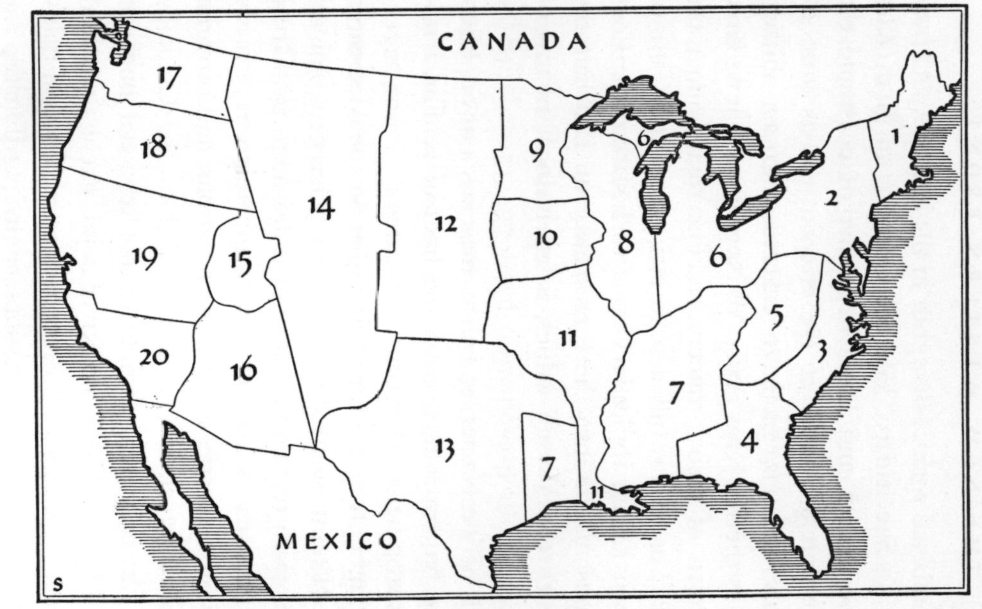

1. Atlantica
2. Hudsonia
3. Piedmont
4. De Soto
5. Appalachia
6. Huron
7. Blue Grass
8. Prairie
9. Superior
10. Cedar
11. Delta
12. Bronco
13. Texahoma
14. Yellowstone
15. Brigham
16. Pueblo
17. Columbia
18. Firland
19. Sierra
20. Angelica

Soto combined against *Bluegrass* in the late war, and beat her badly. She had to cede the Corridor to give *Delta* access to the sea, and also a large strip of coast and the valuable port of Mobile to *DeSoto*. But the dictators of *Bluegrass* and *Huron* have entered into an alliance known as the Ku Klux Axis. All Negroes and Jews have been shorn of their property and banished from these nations. The axis forms a solid strip from the Gulf to the Great Lakes. Its leaders hope to liquidate the Corridor, push *Delta* into the hinterland, and also halt the "Drive to the West," which is an historic policy of *Hudsonia*. Your great nation has long yearned for the oil fields of *Texahoma*, and the wheat fields of Superior. Can she be stopped? It took the lives of a million soldiers to stop her the last time.

Nine nations battle for their rights on the Mississippi River. (Count them on the map.) The geographical unity of this great basin is torn to ribbons by conflicting economic interests. Armies, planes, gunboats, stand ready to back the several claims. Four nations have fought, and will fight again, for the control of the Colorado River. The only thing they can agree upon is a joint war against Mexico. The Ohio River is known as the Rhine of America. Its banks are drenched in the blood of many wars. The navies of five nations, including Canada, dispute the control of the Great Lakes. Submarines lie ready for action in Cleveland, Buffalo, Toronto, Detroit, Windsor, Chicago, Duluth.

Beyond the Lakes, the nations of *Superior*, *Prairie*,

Cedar and their neighbors, have been called the "Balkans of America." They are subject to the acute diplomatic pressure and propaganda of Pan-Canadianism from the vast nation above them (The Great Bear of the North). The goal of Pan-Canadianism is the control of the Mississippi River and the port of New Orleans (A window on the Gulf). As you know, this is also one of the ancestral missions of *Hudsonia.* The unhappy "Balkan" peoples have an agent at each ear.

Little *Brigham* cultivates its irrigated gardens around Great Salt Lake. It is held in affection as being the only nation on the continent ever to pay its war debts. Its state religion, however, is a fertile source of political upheaval. Polygamy shocks and excites the citizens of countries to the east, where the state religion is Methodism.

Columbia and *Firland* in the northwest are at swords' points over fishery and irrigation rights on the Columbia River. Mexico is about to make her fifth great military attempt to reconquer *Texahoma.* Twice she has had it, and twice she has lost it. The minorities problem along the Rio Grande is a simmering volcano.

Down in the southwest corner is the little country of *Angelica.* It has the noisiest artillery, the most resplendent diplomatic corps, and the silkiest female spy system of them all. Its dictator has forty-seven uniforms, and is the only dictator on the continent without an Anti-Semitic policy. A carload of oranges consigned from *Angelica* to *Atlantica* must cross eight armed frontiers (count them) and be inspected, sampled, searched for bombs, checked, cross-checked, double-checked, in duplicate, triplicate, quadruplicate.

Look at the map again. Not one nation of the twenty can feed itself, although a few, like *Cedar*, come near it. Not one but is short of most of the raw materials for its industries. The great *Hudsonia* has coal, but no iron. This she imports from a colony she holds in North Africa. Not one but lives in deadly fear of having its essential supplies cut off by tariffs, embargoes or war. Fearing, they arm to protect their vital interests. Every man, woman and child on the continent has been equipped with a gas mask. They sleep fitfully, these people, for they know not at what hour the sirens will cry their dreadful warning, and New York, Atlanta, Memphis, St. Louis, Denver, Seattle, San Francisco, go down in flames.

II. WE HAVE TIME TO THINK

WE have our problems in the United States, but thank God we do not have *that* problem. Europe has precisely that problem. It follows that the several nations of Europe will continue to get into one jam after another, until somehow they get together. The jams have been bloody and promise to be bloodier. Later we will summarize them in some detail. If there were any way by which the people of the United States could help the people of Europe to get together, perhaps no sacrifice would be too great. But how can we integrate Europe against the violent opposition of most European governments in general, and of British statesmen in particular?

The policy of British statesmen for centuries has been to divide and rule. The last thing they have wanted was a united Europe.

Here is England, here is Germany, here are France, Italy, Japan. Here is the United States of America. Six separate nations; six of the seven great powers. Look at them on a map—a real map this time. What do you see? You see that England and Japan are islands, and not especially large islands. You see that Germany, France and Italy are fragments of the continent of Europe, with boundaries that have little economic justification.

Now look at the United States. It is a clean band, one thousand miles from north to south, straight across the continent of North America. The nightmares of *Hudsonia* and *Angelica* are washed out of it. The waves of the Atlantic come tumbling in on one side, the long rollers of the Pacific on the other. To the south is a big muddy river, and beyond it a dark people of a very ancient culture. This boundary makes some sense. To the north lies more United States in the great territory of Alaska, and an imaginary line, without a gun or a fort along it, beyond which is Canada. It doesn't make much sense, but fortunately it doesn't cause much trouble. Pioneer peoples are on both sides, with a common language.

This broad continental band is far larger than Germany, France, Italy, England and Japan combined. You could put any one of them comfortably in the state of Texas. The band is larger than the whole continent of Europe, outside of Russia. You could put all the twenty-four nations of non-Russian Europe in the United States, and they would take up only two-thirds of the area.

Do you see what I am driving at? It is bound up in that term *United*—the *United* States, the *United* Nations, of America. I am not boasting about how big we are—any tinpot patrioteer can do that. I am trying to emphasize with all my strength the idea that our forty-eight states should not be compared with a single nation in Europe. Iowa cannot go to war with Nebraska. New York cannot raise a tariff wall against Connecticut. In Europe there are twenty-five sovereign states, some of them now bitterly fighting each other, and every one of them with a double-decked, streamlined, copper-riveted tariff wall around it. Every one has a different money system; most have different languages; many have a full complement of armies, navies, generals, ambassadors, bombers, Big Berthas, tanks, torpedoes and unpaid war debts. In the night you can hear the slish of paper, as solemn obligations and treaties are torn up.

There is nothing the matter with the people of Europe. They are fine people, and man for man, probably a grade above Americans in culture, learning and artistic achievement. But the poor devils have never got together since the fall of Rome. They have no European super-state, no federal government, to keep them from bloody quarrels among themselves. The continent is cut up into little fragments, so that no one nation has enough food, coal, iron, copper, oil and what not, for its own needs. These supplies are vital to national survival. If they cannot be assured by peaceful means, they will be seized by military means. And have been, time and again.

Only two regions so far discovered on earth have great deposits of coal, iron and limestone, close enough together to make modern industry feasible on a gigantic scale. Both these regions border on the North Atlantic ocean. One is eastern America, the other is western Europe. The Russians do not have quite such a fortunate combination. They have long costly hauls between their iron, coal and population centers. The American deposits are under one political control. Minnesota does not have to go to war about the coal of West Virginia or Pennsylvania. Iron from Minnesota and coal from Pennsylvania go amiably together into the blast furnaces of Pittsburgh. The European deposits are not under one control. The coal of the Saar Valley, the iron of Lorraine, are not only mineral deposits, they are powder magazines, perpetuating a life and death struggle between Germans and Frenchmen.

We are not a nation in the European sense at all. We have an adequate food supply, and coal, iron, oil, copper and most of the essential raw materials for industry, snug within our own borders. The only nation in similar circumstances is Russia. But Russia does not have 3,000 miles of salt water between herself and the seething states of Europe. She seethes[1] right into Finland, Poland, Latvia, Rumania and Turkey. Russia does not have 5,000 miles of salt water between herself and Japan, as we do. Manchukuo simmers close beside her. Border skirmishes have been going on for years, and in the summer of 1939 pitched battles were fought in Manchukuo and outer Mongolia. Vladivostok is within bombing range of Tokyo—and vice versa.

The United States is different in kind from any other nation on the planet, except Russia. It is different from

[1] This is a horrible example of the vice of personifying names of nations. Elsewhere in the book I have tried to avoid such meaningless expressions. Where for brevity I have had to use the name of a nation as symbol for that nation's government or army or geographic area, I have tried to make the context show clearly which aspect is meant.

Russia in an important *space* dimension–being separated by oceans from Europe and Asia; and in an important *time* dimension–being much further along the road of industrial development.

The United States is unique and alone. It does not have to act the way less fortunate nations are forced to act. Its statesmen do not have to copy the policies of other countries in respect to war, alliances, foreign trade, loans abroad, competitive intrigue, colonies, outlets for surplus populations. It lacks certain material conditions which produced Communism in Russia, Fascism in Italy, Naziism in Germany, aggressive militarism in Japan. To import these ideologies to America is like importing crushed stone to burn in a furnace–they make no sense under our conditions.

We are free from the administrative difficulties of the British Empire, sprawled over the seven seas and threaded together by precarious "lifelines." When Mussolini threatened the line to India in 1935, over the matter of oil sanctions, the British had to fight or back down. They backed down, I suppose, because the "rights of small nations," as exemplified by Ethiopia, were not worth the risk of cutting the lifeline in the Mediterranean. English statesmen have to look at least ten ways at once. No wonder they get crosseyed. Our only remote possession of importance is the Philippine Islands. They cost us more than we got out of them. We are wisely arranging to let them go.

The people of the United States are, to put it modestly, on a par with the people of Europe in technical methods for producing goods. We make better Fords; they make better Rolls Royces.

The people of the United States are one hundred and fifty years ahead of the people of Europe in political and economic unity. We ended our career as a group of quarreling nations, and began our career as an integrated continent in 1789. Twenty years later, Napoleon tried to launch Europe on a similar career, but English statesmen and generals would not have it. They stopped a possible United States of Europe at Waterloo.

THE NEW WAR

In the "new world war," as it is ominously called, there is going to be much controversy over the rôle of the United States, and almost certainly a determined attempt to enlist our material and military aid. Twenty nations in Europe are still neutral at this writing. More than half of them are written off by the belligerents as permanent neutrals, not to be asked for a single soldier. No one says Switzerland is helping Hitler or failing to stand by democracy if Switzerland does not declare war on Germany. Yet gun for gun, dollar for dollar, and man for man, Swiss resources on the German border would be more effective than American resources 3,000 miles away.

If our government does its duty it will protect our national interest regardless of the claims of other powers. Where does our national interest lie? Citizens need to be very clear in their minds about this. In Chapter XI we shall discuss it at more length.

We need not be involved if we are clear enough about our purpose. We shall feel the effects of the war, of course, even more than we feel them already; and we shall have to adjust and readjust almost all our plans and activities to the tragic events. We shall need to keep our heads in the midst of a barrage of propaganda and slogans.

If Belgium and Holland, Denmark and Switzerland, or any one of these countries, can guard the imaginary line of its frontier with Germany and keep neutral, are we going to throw up our hands and say we can't stay out? It would be more honest to say we don't want to stay out.

Twenty-two years ago we cheered loudly for a phrase, and marched out to make the world "safe for democracy." There are fewer nations with a democratic form of government in the world today than in 1914. We helped to make possible, through the vindictive terms of the Treaty of Versailles, that sterling pair of democrats, Mussolini and Hitler. Perhaps there are similar boomerangs in some of the phrases loose today. Certainly it will do no harm to crack them open and examine them carefully before marching off in all directions to make the world safe for something.

People in other countries may have no time to crack anything open before their own skulls are cracked. They are forced to stop thinking and begin fighting.

We can wait. We can think. We can choose a course. Here on our broad continent, with salt water to east and west, we have a chance to see what is best to be done—best for ourselves, best for the world.

We cannot think or choose without facts to guide us. If we trust to swinging phrases and surging emotions, we are likely to send our young men off to save something again; and whether it is the Polish Corridor, or the British Empire, or the Standard Oil Company, or Mr. Morgan's pocketbook, we may not find out till years later.

Let us look at some of the outstanding facts which bear on this situation. I will try not to clutter them up with too many personal conclusions. I want the facts to be useful, even if you come to different conclusions. The guns are roaring at this moment. It took less than three years after the guns roared at Liége in 1914 before we were in a war which won us nothing, won the world nothing, and cost us much. Most of us do not want to be rushed off our feet again. We do not need to be if we have some solid knowledge to brace our feet upon.

III. SOME EASTERN FRONTS

WE know two facts about European politics, and we are always forgetting them. One is that we can never hope to understand its diplomatic secrets. No matter how many cards the great statesmen lay on the table, they always keep a few up their sleeves. The other fact is that European governments act from considerations of power and national interest, not from the high principles that embellish their public documents.

Let us look at the background of the current war and observe some of the issues and alleged issues. If you point out that I am not a specialist in European diplomacy, I can answer that I know something of its economic objectives. Or I can answer that I have seen high officials of our State Department thoroughly nonplused by events in Europe. Or I can answer that I am making a study of the issues for which my son might be ordered to go and fight.

Graham Hutton, a former editor of the London *Economist*, says in his *Survey After Munich:* "What we have seen between 1933 and 1938 in Europe . . . is only part of an historical struggle between national forces in a crowded continent—crowded not in the sense of being over-populated, but in the sense of harboring tribes and nations with conflicting aims in a very narrow space. If those nations could only agree to sink their differences, to lower the wall of armaments and tariffs along their borders, to eliminate in effect all frontiers, and to bend their energies towards mutual understanding . . . the result might well be that Europe . . . would find itself terribly under-populated."

In the days of muskets, various nations in Europe could at least feed themselves. When a prince was seized with a desire to acquire territory and declared war on his neighbors, populations could not readily be starved out. The power age and the factory system have changed all that by greatly enlarging the area capable of self-support. Mr. Hutton says that if Germany should succeed in annexing Rumania, Hungary, Yugo-Slavia, Bulgaria, Turkey, Greece, as well as Austria, Czechoslovakia and Poland, she would still be short of many essential raw materials.

In another generation, the trend may be reversed again through the invention of chemical substitutes, as we shall see in Chapter VII. But the day when any one nation in Europe cannot only feed itself, but supply its factories, is far in the future. Up to now, industrial development has tended to forge Europe into a single technological organism, linked with railroads, power lines, telephones, airways, motor roads, and active exchange of raw materials and finished goods.

Yet across this technological and commercial unity rise the boundaries of national states, with their custom houses and Maginot lines. Nationalist orators boast about the invincible self-sufficiency, the indomitable will, of

France or Poland or Germany. The brute facts of technological development reduce these brave words to so much static. If Germany cannot obtain vast stocks of raw materials abroad, she cannot feed her people, much less wage a prolonged war. The sovereign nations of Europe have made little economic sense for generations; in 1940 they make none.

The German tanks, trucks and airplanes overran most of Poland in a few days. In the time of Frederick the Great, the ox-paced armies would have wallowed back and forth for months or years. Modern science not only makes European boundaries obsolete economically, it has made Europe an almost impossible home for anybody when a general war breaks out. Even the threat of war throws Europeans into a justifiable panic. When are the airplanes coming; when will the bombs begin to fall? What can we do to save the children; where can grandfather go? Instead of flocking to the protection of city walls, people flee to the country from cities which may become smoking ruins or gas-filled traps. Air attack on a great modern city has still not shown its full power.

Men, women and children are being killed by mass production, by remote electrical controls, by the latest discoveries from chemical laboratories. Mechanical improvements in the art of sudden death have made notable progress during the twenty-one-year armistice which ended on September 1, 1939. Not far from a quarter of a trillion dollars' worth of armament has been accumulated in the period, supported by research of unparalleled precision. The arms are piled up now mountain high, ready to be touched off. Every government in Europe has contributed to this overhanging mountain. A little toppled down, and Poland ceased to exist as a nation. Let the whole mass slide, and Europe may cease to exist except for cavemen.

Humans are the only race of animals that organize to kill their kind. When the killing is instructed by the laboratory, the ratio of efficiency becomes very high. Cathedrals, museums, universities, the fruit of centuries of patient advance, are destroyed. Not only do the living die, but the children who might have been, die too. In these phantom graves, how many great artists, scientists, poets of the future, lie buried?

The people of Europe are not unused to the horrors of war. They have faced and met them again and again. *Today they face the question of survival.* The conflict of nations in this war is of little moment compared to the contest between the population and the mountain of armament.

REAL ESTATE AND HIGH PRINCIPLES

On March 10, 1939, Joseph Stalin said to the Communist Party Congress: "An open redivision of the world and of spheres of influence is taking place before our eyes at the expense of non-aggressor states." On August twenty-first the announcement of the first of Stalin's treaties with Germany indicated that he wanted a cut in this redivision. But the shifts began earlier; in

1917 at Brest-Litovsk, when Germany took a slice out of Russia, and in 1919 at Versailles, when France and England recarved Germany and Austria.

In the United States, when real estate changes hands, the individual deeding it does not expect to repossess. He takes his money and that is that. There may be lawsuits, backbiting and spite fences, for emotions run high in land quarrels, but transfers depend on reasonable compensation. The same is true in Europe so far as individual ownership goes. But over and above transfers between citizens, stand the super-transfers of national territory, won and lost in war. Apparently no nation gives up a vested interest in lands it once collected taxes from. The Poles used to own Poland and still consider the territory theirs. But Russia and Germany owned most of Poland from 1796 to 1919. Now the latter have taken it back as a matter of "national justice," but it is safe to say that the Poles will never acknowledge the claim.

Europe is like a big real estate market in which hardly any title is clear, and every nation which has ever occupied a given section lays claim to it in perpetuity, "bought by the blood of heroes." This makes for a real estate situation even wilder than the Florida boom. Men fight and die for a few parcels of land, and how good is the title when the property is transferred? In such a market, how can permanent boundary lines ever be established? The answer is, they can't. Only a United States of Europe can solve this problem, as Mr. Hutton says.

We are assured by idealists that nothing so crass as real estate is involved in the present clash between Hitlerism and democracy. They tell us it is a war of principle, a struggle between right and wrong. Hitler's methods of taking title to what he considers the lands of his fathers infuriate me. His treatment of minorities within his own country would be envied by Caligula. His voice over the radio makes me want to choke him. But I cannot choke him and I cannot find any lofty principles clear-cut enough to warrant my killing German bookkeepers and farmhands in an attempt to settle with Hitler.

In 1917 we were told that if we fought for the Allies we should help to end war forever, abolish autocracy, protect the rights of small nations, and insure open covenants, openly arrived at. But our Allies had secret treaties up their sleeves. This was a great disillusion.

We were told that the League of Nations was going to maintain the peace of the world; that its power to declare economic sanctions would stop aggressors in their tracks. Many of us were hopeful that this was so. But when Mussolini proposed to take title to Ethiopia, France and England, through the Hoare-Laval agreement, cynically broke the united front of League sanctions, and presented Mussolini with the Empire of the Negus.

We were told that France and England would stand by their solemn pledges to protect the integrity of Czechoslovakia. At Munich, Messrs. Chamberlain and

Daladier sold this nice little country down the river—as the commentators put it.

We were solemnly promised by Mr. Hitler that after acquiring the Sudetenland he had "no further territorial demands to make on Europe." Hardly were the words out of his mouth before he had scooped up Memel and the rest of Czechoslovakia.

We were told that Hitler was a tool of the capitalists. He turned out to be one of their worst enemies, practically abolishing private initiative in Germany.

We were told that the Loyalists in Spain were the last defense of democracy. We were warned that if General Franco won, the Lord help France when she should go to war with Germany. Franco would attack on one side while Germany attacked from the other. We believers in democracy were worried and contributed large sums to the Loyalist cause. But now we find that Franco is furious with Germany for signing the pact with Russia, and is growing more friendly with the embattled democracies every day.

We were most solemnly assured by qualified experts that, whatever happened, Russia would always oppose Hitler. Communism could not compromise with fascism. (Hitler said this, too, but the other way around.) On August 10, 1939, a broadside by four hundred American intellectuals said that "Soviet and fascist policies are diametrically opposed" and that anyone who bracketed Russia and Germany was a reactionary "attempting to split the democratic front." Vincent Sheean, Max Lerner and Frederick L. Schuman were among those who assured us of the undying enmity of Stalin for Hitler. Imagine our surprise when the boys began to make a wedding cake out of Poland.

The moral is not so much to seek better information—for who knows which way a Stalin, a Hitler, a Chamberlain is going to jump?—as to distrust firmly all great principles of right and wrong invoked for or against European nations. Who says he is on the side of the angels, and who wrote his speech?

Most of the foregoing questions have been answered by history. Here are a few more still unanswered as I write. Some of them are mysteries which may never be solved. To others the Allied governments owe us an answer before we turn out our pockets for them again.

1. Was Hitler bluffing at Munich or would he have marched into Czechoslovakia?

2. Would he have marched into Poland without the Russian pact?

3. Did that understudy of Metternich, Herr von Ribbentrop, gamble too far on Mr. Chamberlain's eagerness for friendship with Germany? That is, did he assure Hitler in 1939 as he had in 1938 that the British were only bluffing?

4. *Were* the British bluffing? Did each side call the other's bluff?

5. Would Mr. Chamberlain have declared war if he had not feared that his cabinet would fall? Did he intend on Saturday, September second, to declare war? Did he

contemplate a sort of token war, to be ended by agreeing to possible Italian peace terms after the Poles were liquidated?

6. Did the British government ever seriously intend to help the Poles? If not, why did it promise aid in so emphatic a treaty, which angered Hitler and perhaps helped to provoke the war? If the English *did* intend to help the Poles, why did they hold up a comparatively small loan for tanks and airplanes? Why did they advise the Poles against mobilizing? Why did they not contribute some aid against the German air force?

7. Why did the English return Czechoslovak funds to the Germans in the summer of 1939?

8. Will the Russians supply Germany with food, oil and other materials? Can they spare enough? Will they supply them on credit? If they do, will they have more success in collecting than the United States did from her Allies after the last war?

9. What price did Stalin demand if he should join England and France to guarantee Poland?

10. What price did Stalin extract from Hitler?

11. How much pre-1914 territory does Stalin want back, and at whose cost?

12. Is the policy of Pan-Slavism being revived? How long can it be reconciled with Pan-Germanism?

13. Are the Russians executing a double double-cross on Hitler by blocking his path in the Balkans?

14. Did they secretly guarantee Rumania against German attack? If not, how did King Carol dare to purge his local Nazis on September 22, 1939?

15. What offers have the Allies made to Italy since the war began?

16. How strong is the Right opposition against Hitler? Had the German generals any plan to overthrow him, either before Munich or after the invasion of Poland?

17. How many Fuehrers can live peacefully side by side in Europe, each pledged to the idea that he is the whole show?

18. Lacking an international police and Supreme Court, is there any way to change boundaries except by armed force? Will any beneficiary of the status quo consent to give up real estate by negotiations?

19. Is there any dependable protection for the rights of small nations? Is there any way to assure self-determination for minorities within a nation? Suppose there are minorities inside the minorities, like a nest of little boxes? (See the next chapter.)

20. Suppose the Allies again defeat Germany and dictate a peace treaty like Versailles. Is there any way you can keep eighty million industrious, intelligent people permanently crushed without slaughtering them all? And what kind of a great moral crusade do you call that?

The territories on the western side of the Atlantic are not troubled with questions of this character. That is why some forty million people left the eastern side during the last century to come to America. Do they, or their sons and grandsons, want to go back again? Today we are again invited to subscribe to lofty principles of right and wrong in Europe, and back them with expeditionary forces and armed might. Shall we fight, then:

Against totalitarianism—with our allies already forced into rigid military dictatorships, and with the M Day program of our own War Department (see Chapter XI) ready to be clamped down upon us if we go in?

Against fascism—perhaps with the father of fascism as our ally? Britain and France are apparently leaving no stone unturned to win Mussolini to their side.

Against communism—when it is not impossible that Stalin may do another back somersault and land in the Allies' camp? Believe me, all would be forgiven Mr. Stalin if he did.

Against aggression—hand in hand with the conquerors of India, Africa and Asia Minor? The British and French Empires were built on aggressive imperialism. So was the United States.

Against threats to international law and the freedom of the seas—with the Allies already practicing search and seizure of neutral vessels in their rigorous blockade of Germany?

Against treaty breakers—with the former guarantors of Czechoslovakia?

If we must fight, let us find out this time for what we are really fighting. If this can be uncovered beneath the frosting of lofty principles, it is extremely probable that we shall not need to fight at all.

IV. AN INVENTORY OF EUROPE

IN the last 2,500 years, there has probably been more blood spilled in Europe than in the rest of the world combined. Being richer and more civilized than other continents, it has been able to afford bigger and better wars. Consider the procession—the Greek wars and Alexander the Great; the Roman wars and Caesar the Great; the wars of the Middle Ages and Charlemagne the Great; the dynastic wars of Spain, Austria, England, France, Holland, Prussia, Sweden, Russia, and Frederick and Peter the Great; the wars which followed the French Revolution and Napoleon the Great; the World War of 1914 and Nobody the Great. Moors have fought Christians, Catholics have fought Protestants, Slavs have fought Teutons, Englishmen have fought Spaniards, Frenchmen, Germans, Irishmen. Swedes have fought Germans, "fascists" have fought "communists," "democracies" have fought "autocracies."

After the fall of Rome, Europe broke up into petty tribal states dominated by twopenny war lords—something like China before 1937. The Catholic Church offered a kind of religious unity, but there was little economic unity. Dante dreamed of one king and one spiritual ruler for Europe. He was at least 700 years ahead of his time. The little feudal states grew into duchies, ruled by a duke; principalities, ruled by a prince; kingdoms, ruled by a king. These fragments were divided, combined and handed around with little respect for race, language, geography or trade. The common people fed the princelings and their retainers, and paid the costs as usual.

The idea of a "nation" in the modern sense was unknown. There was no concept of "national honor," patriotism, international law, the "family of nations," freedom of the seas. People gave their allegiance to the lord, not to the country and flag. "To a man of the Middle Ages," says Charles A. Beard, "his 'country' meant little more than the neighborhood in which he lived." "Nationalism" as we know it did not make its appearance until the downfall of feudalism and the rise of the commercial state, along about 1600. Remember this. Nationalism is not a fixed, eternal principle, something like the law of gravitation. It is a comparative newcomer as human institutions go. It crept into men's minds only about three hundred years ago. It is not impossible that it might creep out again.

As the kingdoms grew stronger, the idea of "dynastic interest" came to the fore. This meant that the ruler was a kind of god—"The King can do no wrong." Great ruling families established themselves—the Medicis, Bourbons, Hapsburgs, Tudors, the House of Hanover, the Romanoffs, the Hohenzollerns. Vestiges of this quaint notion can still be found. It created the news value in King Edward's abdication and marriage to Mrs. Simpson. The Kaiser tried to rally the royal houses of Europe in support of Spain, in the Spanish-American War of 1898. He didn't get much action because the other dynasties were growing feeble. A pretender to the throne boldly entered France after the peace of Munich. Spain may not yet be through with the house of Hapsburg.

Time and again a strong monarch would make a bid for the mastery of Europe. England, content with her island isolation and her overseas dominions, always opposed him. English statesmen did not want any one great power on the continent. The Channel is only twenty miles wide. Their disapproval took the form of alliances and counter-alliances with the Strong Man's enemies. Successive alliances were made to put down Charles V, Philip II, Louis XIV, Napoleon and Wilhelm II. It was a policy which English business men, controlling parliament, followed as zealously as had the earlier English kings.

British statesmen fomented discord among the thirteen American states after the Revolution. Other British statesmen aided a group of despots to put a despot on the throne of France, after the downfall of Napoleon. They backed the South in our Civil War; for one reason, *two* American nations looked safer to them than a single great nation. They blocked a possible rapprochement between Russia and Germany in 1906, by bribing Russia with the partition of Persia. Meanwhile Englishmen's love of liberty has not shown itself to best advantage in Ireland, India, Egypt, in the attack on the Boers, the Chinese Opium War, the partition of Zanzibar in cahoots with Germany. The Versailles treaty, the Spanish civil war, Munich, and post-Munich dealings tell a similar story. Jerome Frank puts it strongly: "Unless and until Europe rids itself of that English-fomented European disunity, America is helpless in the task of helping Europe or of promoting world peace."

I am not disposed to cast aspersions at British statesmen—especially in view of what American statesmen and marines have done in the Caribbean from time to time. All I desire is to point out that great moral crusades—for democracy, world peace, international law, freedom of the seas—with our British cousins, should not be undertaken until these facts have been given due consideration. It is not our mission, as I see it, to retrieve the mistakes of the British Empire, or any other empire.

PRINCIP'S REVOLVER

On June 28, 1914, Franz Ferdinand, heir to the throne of Austria, is driving through the streets of Serajevo, the capital of Bosnia. Bosnia is a small Slavic province in the Balkans which Austria annexed in 1909. The people of Bosnia do not want to be annexed by Austria, they want to join Serbia. Serbs and Bosnians hate Austrians. Suddenly a young man named Princip appears at the side of the carriage, with a drawn revolver. He belongs to a secret society of Slavic patriots. He fires pointblank at Franz Ferdinand and kills him.

The rulers of Austria, scenting a political plot, send an ultimatum to the Serbian government. Russia backs up

Serbia. Are they not both Slavic peoples? A week of frantic diplomacy follows—without radio accompaniment. Who is going to back whom? Secret treaties have already settled the question, but since they are secret, diplomats are only sure about their own dark commitments, not about the other fellow's. Troops begin to fill the streets on their way to barracks. Germany backs Austria, and presently Bulgaria and Turkey do likewise. France supports Russia—her bankers have been loaning billions of francs to the Czar. England, after some painful hesitations, backs France. Russia mobilizes. Austria mobilizes. France and Germany mobilize. Italy is supposed to back Austria, but it develops later that she has a secret treaty with France. When promised a fat slice of Austria, she joins the Allies in 1915. Germany tears up her treaty covering Belgian neutrality—the famous "scrap of paper"—her gray-clad army swings across the frontier, and the Great War is on. By August 5, the British navy has dredged up and cut all cables running from Germany to America. Hereafter we shall get practically all our news from one side.

By 1914, many of the small nations of Europe had been consolidated into powerful empires. Germany had been unified under Bismarck, and the Kaiser was looking for territory and trade. His generals and business men had sold him the idea of vigorous expansion to the east, with the aid of the Austro-Hungarian Empire—the "Drang nach Osten." Beyond the Balkans lay Constantinople, and beyond the Golden Horn lay Bagdad. It was an appealing picture of imperial destiny. But it was also a direct challenge to the Russian and British Empires. To check it, Russia had been stirring up the Slavs in the Balkans to revolt against Austria. Two wars had been fought, in 1911 and 1912. Meanwhile French schoolboys had been fired with *revanche* for the provinces of Alsace and Lorraine, lost to Germany in the war of 1870.

Germans feared the Russian bear on the east and the British navy on the west. They felt encircled by two mighty foes. Nor was France what you might call neighborly. An armament race was going hell bent, as it is today—armies, navies, fortifications—but no airplanes. This is important. When the news of approaching battle was known in Berlin and Paris, the people went wild shouting "War! War!" and "On to Berlin!" When the news of approaching battle was known in London, Paris, Warsaw, Berlin, in September, 1939, the people were quiet. Few cried for war; most of them watched the sky. The standing armies of Europe totaled 5,000,000 men in 1914. Germany was collecting colonies in Africa and colliding with British and French colonial interests. The exporters of goods and of capital in each Empire were engaged in an ever more desperate economic war.

Into this explosive mixture a spark fell from the revolver of Gavrilo Princip. An explosion would have come anyway. Tensions were unbearable. The final cost, as you know, was 20,000,000 dead, mountains of wealth destroyed, political democracy thrust backward, and a world economic system disabled beyond repair.

President Wilson hoped to end the war with a just and lasting peace. Some say he was a fool to try. Few know that *he* knew it was probably hopeless. On the night before the United States entered the war, he talked to Frank I. Cobb in the White House. He didn't want to recommend war; he knew that he must, and he foresaw the tragic outcome with the utmost clarity. He said: "Once lead this people into war, and they'll forget there was ever such a thing as tolerance. To fight you must be brutal and ruthless, and the spirit of ruthless brutality will enter into the very fiber of our national life, infecting Congress, the courts, the policeman on the beat, the man on the street. . . . Yes, it means that we will lose our heads along with the rest, and stop weighing right and wrong. . . . It means an attempt to reconstruct a peacetime civilization with war standards, and at the end of the war there will be no by-standers with sufficient power to influence the terms. There won't be any peace standards left to work with. There will be only war standards."

He tried to do his best, hoping against hope. He announced the Fourteen Points. The Germans laid down their arms—after they were pretty well beaten, to be sure—and asked for the application of the Fourteen Points. Mr. Clemenceau, virtual dictator of France, rolled an eye to Heaven: "Even God," he said, "was satisfied with Ten Commandments, but Wilson insists on

Fourteen." By and large, that was the view of Mr. Lloyd George. President Wilson left the conference table in Paris to go home, bitter and defeated. What he had foreseen on that terrible night in the White House had come true. A similar disappointment awaits anyone who follows his course.

CLEMENCEAU'S TREATY

The Treaty of Versailles covered 230 large pages. The German government was commanded to pay a thirty-three billion dollar war indemnity over a period of years. The Allies then took her trade, her colonies, sections of her home territory, and a large share of her moveables, in the shape of horses, cows, ships and locomotives. She didn't have anything left to pay with. The French army occupied the Ruhr Valley, seized factories, imprisoned mayors and booted citizens around. Poor debtors get rough treatment everywhere. Presently the great German currency inflation arrived, a direct effect of the Treaty. A cup of coffee cost 100,000,000 marks.

Then came the Dawes Plan and the Young Plan. Brisk American financiers were going to fix everything. The thirty-three billion was scaled down to eight billion—real money. It might as well have been scaled up to eight hundred billion—for Germany could not export enough goods to pay more than a small fraction of eight billion dollars. In a few years the Young Plan blew up, and President Hoover proposed a moratorium on all indemnity payments in 1931. The Allies said that if Germany couldn't pay indemnities to *them*, they couldn't pay their war debts to the United States. The United States government said that reparations and war debts were two separate questions and should not be confused. Mr. Coolidge said: "They hired the money."

Italy did not get that large slice of Austria she had been promised for deserting her alliance with Austria. She got only a little slice. So she went in and seized the port of Fiume anyway. Her statesmen and people felt humiliated and cheated—ripe ground for an enterprising ex-Socialist agitator named Benito Mussolini.

Europe was distraught enough in 1914, with some twenty sovereign states competing for markets, raw materials and political power. The Treaty made seven new ones—Poland, Czechoslovakia, Finland, Estonia, Latvia, Hungary and Lithuania. Serbia became Yugo-Slavia, with many additional trimmings. Poland and Czechoslovakia promptly entered the race for markets, raw materials and power. Seven thousand miles of new tariff walls were erected. Minorities everywhere began to cry for Mr. Wilson's self-determination. It was a lofty principle but it made little sense in the economic realities of the twentieth century. It cut across railways, waterways, highways, power lines, natural trading areas.

Let us follow J. F. Horrabin in a brief inventory of the cleavages in modern Europe. Some of them existed before the war, many were added by the Treaty. As you go down the list, try to imagine similar situations in the United States.

EUROPE SEPTEMBER, 1939

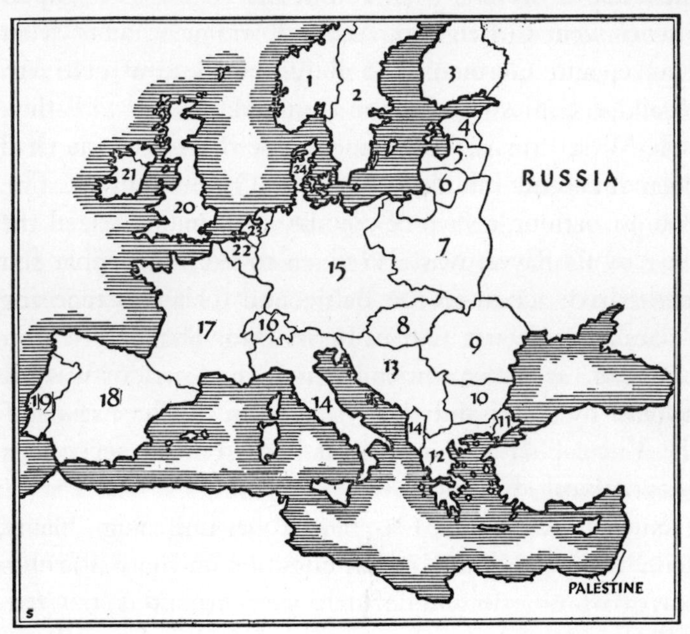

1. Norway
2. Sweden
3. Finland
4. Estonia
5. Latvia
6. Lithuania
7. Poland (September 15, 1939)
8. Hungary
9. Rumania
10. Bulgaria
11. Turkey
12. Greece
13. Yugo-Slavia
14. Italy and Albania
15. Greater Germany
16. Switzerland
17. France
18. Spain
19. Portugal
20. England
21. Irish Free State
22. Belgium
23. Holland
24. Denmark

The Treaty makers took an enormous pair of shears and clipped Germany all round the edges. The Eupen district went to Belgium. Alsace-Lorraine went back to France, and German schoolboys could now cultivate *revanche*. Schleswig went to Denmark, Memel to Lithuania, West Prussia, Posen and Upper Silesia to the new Poland, another chunk of Silesia to Czechoslovakia. The Polish Corridor, a strip of country fifty miles wide along the Vistula River, was also given to Poland, so that she might have access to the Baltic Sea. This was nice for Poland, but it cut Germany in two. But before you weep for Germany, remember that the Corridor was inhabited by Poles and that "the Poles are the nation of the Vistula." If Hitler takes it back, Poland becomes a geographical absurdity.

Russia lost Finland, Estonia, Latvia, Lithuania, Poland and Bessarabia. The Russian coastline on the Baltic was narrowed to a miserable little strip around Petrograd. The Treaty of Versailles confirmed the Treaty of Brest-Litovsk which Lenin had signed earlier with a victorious Germany in the East. Revel and Riga on the Baltic are natural railheads for traffic from the vast interior of Russia. They were bottled up by the creation of Estonia and Latvia.

Poland was carved out of Germany, Russia, Austro-Hungary and the Ukraine. Poland has been getting carved and recarved for centuries. In 1920 a Polish army raided Lithuania and seized Vilna. Lithuania retaliated by closing the Niemen River and Memel to Poland.

Austria-Hungary lost the provinces of Galicia, Bohemia, Moravia, East Hungary, Transylvania, Southern Tyrol, Istria, Croatia, Dalmatia and Bosnia-Herzegovina. The gainers, besides Poland, were Czechoslovakia, Rumania, Italy and Yugo-Slavia. The Austrian Empire had a population of 51,000,000 in 1914. After the shearing operation only 15,000,000 remained—less than 7,000,000 in a tiny Austria, and 8,000,000 in a severely emaciated Hungary. Austria was composed principally of the city of Vienna—all head and no body. Small wonder it fell easily to Hitler. The Empire had seaports on the Adriatic. The new Austria, the new Hungary, became landlocked states.

Bulgaria was the strongest nation in the Balkans in 1912. After the shears went to work she became the weakest. Choice morsels were thrown to Yugo-Slavia, Greece and Rumania. Greece was also given a slice of Turkey, including some in Asia Minor. This led to another war in 1921, and the Greeks were forced to abandon Asia Minor.

While we are in Asia Minor let us look at Palestine. It is a country about as big as Vermont. England was given mandatory power over it by the Treaty. Jews are said to be good judges of property, but the Zionist leaders must have been thinking of something else when they picked Palestine. Anne O'Hare McCormick sizes it up: "The Jews have found a homeland about as peaceful as the live crater of a volcano." It is the crossroads of three world religions, Mohammedanism, Judaism, Christianity.

It is a bloody battlefield between Arabs and Jews for land and political power. The Arabs are under pressure from Germany and Italy on the one side, and from England on the other. It is the crossroads of the British life-line to the Near East, and the oil fields of Iraq and Persia. "Jerusalem has become again a focus of the assorted creeds and clashing faiths of the world."

A map of minorities in Europe is enough to turn your hair white. We must never forget that these minorities are not *racial* in any biological sense. The people of Europe are so mixed up by migration, intermarriage, marchings and counter-marchings, for three thousand years, that it is impossible to locate a well-defined race, as any competent anthropologist will tell you, unless employed by Hitler.

The characteristics which distinguish minorities are chiefly language, religion, local customs and peasant dress. Close their mouths, strip them, shave their heads, and you could hardly tell an Irishman from a Croat. Incidentally, it is difficult to find two nations in Europe with the same language. The Belgians speak French officially, and that is about all.

Poland has minorities of White Russians, Ruthenians, Ukrainians and Jews. Yugo-Slavia has Serbs, Croats and Slovenes. No love is lost between the Serbs, who are Greek Orthodox, and the Croats, who are Catholic. Fear of Germany has united them for the moment but the union may fall apart at any time. Rumania has Hungarians, Ukrainians and Jews. Bulgaria has Turks,

Greeks, and a Macedonian "irredentist" group with a permanent blood feud with Yugo-Slavia. Germany has Czechs, Jews and Viennese; Lithuania has Russians, Poles and Jews; Latvia has ditto and Germans; Hungary has Germans and Slovaks; Greece has Rumanians, Macedonians and Turks; Italy has Germans in the Tyrol. The Turks used to sit heavily on Bulgarians, Greeks and Syrians, but now, alas, sit only on Kurds. Switzerland is compounded of Germans, Italians and French. Walloons and Flemings call each other bitter names in Belgium. Spain has been split not only among fascists, communists, Trotskyites, anarchists, democrats, liberals, Catholics and anti-Catholics, but among Castilians, Galicians, Basques and Catalonians. Ireland simmers between the Catholics of the Free State and the Protestants of Ulster. Only Sweden and Norway seem to lack a minorities problem.

Now as to a few economic cleavages. Remember that each state has a frontier armed with guns and tariff walls. Here is the River Rhine. With its tributaries it forms a natural economic area and a transport system for the great coal and iron deposits and industrial establishments which lie in the basin. The Rhine rises in Switzerland. Then it runs for 100 miles in France—that is, one bank is in France. Then for 300 miles it runs in Germany. Then for 100 miles in Holland, where it flows to the sea beyond Rotterdam. Five nations contest this basin—Germany, France, Belgium, Holland, Switzerland.

Here is the beautiful blue Danube. Austrian Germany,

Hungary, Yugo-Slavia, and Rumania cut it to pieces. Before the war, it flowed inside the Austro-Hungarian Empire for 700 miles, and made some sense. Hitler may at least revive that type of geographic sense. It is interesting to recall that when the Austro-German Customs Union was launched after the war with the object of bringing unity and stability into the Danube basin, French bankers killed it.

The Mediterranean boils with rival national interests. Here converge the British lifeline to India, the French lifeline to Africa, the Spanish lifeline to Morocco, the Italian lifeline to Ethiopia, the British and French lines to Syria and the Near East, the lifeline from Greece to Crete, the route of bottled-up Russia out of the Black Sea. Since Munich, Italian mobs have shouted for Corsica, Nice and Tunisia, long held by France. French mobs have shouted for Sardinia, long held by Italy. Seven sovereign powers abut on this inland sea, each with an ax to grind, while Germany, Russia and England have a heavy stake in its destiny. How soundly should we sleep if the Caribbean were girdled with seven powerful and jealous nations, armed to the hilt?

A list of the political persuasions of the various European governments is worth attention. It is compiled as of September, 1939, and subject to change without notice:

Political Democracies	*Dictatorships—90%* *Pure*
England	Poland
Irish Free State	Lithuania

Political Democracies (Continued)	*Dictatorships—90% Pure (Continued)*
France	Latvia
Belgium	Estonia
Holland	Hungary
Switzerland	Rumania
Denmark	Yugo-Slavia
Norway	Bulgaria
Sweden	Greece
Finland	Turkey
	Portugal

Dictatorships—100% Pure

Greater Germany	Russia
Italy	Spain

The inventory of European cleavages recited above is far from complete, but it gives the general idea. Just to round out the picture, we will present Hitler's program as set forth in his book, *Mein Kampf*.

1. Return of German colonies in Africa and the Pacific. (Not yet)
2. Recapture of the Rhineland. (Check)
3. Recapture of the Saar Valley. (Check)
4. Recapture of Danzig. (Check)
5. Recapture of the Polish Corridor. (Check)
6. Recapture of Memel. (Check)
7. Recapture of Upper Silesia. (Check)
8. The absorption of Austria. (Check)
9. The fortification of the Rhine. (Check—the Siegfried Line)

10. The neutrality of England. (No)

11. Alliance with Italy. (Yes and no)

12. Alliance with Japan. (Yes and no)

13. A fascist Spain, with access to her mineral resources. (Check)

14. The removal of Czechoslovakia. (Check)

15. The domination of eastern Europe. (Well?)

16. The "liberation" of Germans in Switzerland, Holland, Denmark and the Tyrol. (Not yet)

17. The seizure of the Ukraine. (Doubtful)

v. HOME AGAIN

WE now board a steamship and come back to the United States. We land in New York. New York is full of minorities—Italians, Negroes, Greeks, Poles, Czechs, Germans, Jews. They get into scuffles occasionally, but the melting pot melts in spite of them. Their children go to the public schools and learn English. Their daughters buy dresses at Klein's which look like Bonwit Teller's from across the street. Their sons play baseball, drive cars, dance the Jitterbug, and say: Oh, yeah. Americans, see? Few immigrants have come in for ten years now. From 1820 to 1930, 38 million came in.

No group, even when living in a foreign "quarter" and speaking no English, dreams of demanding self-determination. That's what they came to get away from. Can you imagine Jews in New York asking autonomy for the Bronx? No group is crying to be repatriated in Canada, in Cuba or Mexico, taking a slice of American territory along with it. No call has come from the Negroes of Alabama for the setting up of the sovereign state of Cottonland. (A call was recently heard, however, in our colony of Puerto Rico, but the Puerto Ricans are quiet for the moment.)

In 1776, the people of thirteen provinces on the eastern coast of North America decided they had had enough of the dynasts of Europe—especially the House of Hanover. They got out their squirrel rifles and attacked the British army of occupation at Lexington, Concord and Bunker Hill. A planter from Virginia named George Washington was given command of the rebellious sharpshooters. He fought the British up and down the colonies for seven years. He didn't know when he was beaten. Finally, with some help from the French, and to the amazement of the world, he won the fight. General Cornwallis handed over his sword.

The colonies were now free to govern themselves. They were not, however, a united country. They were thirteen little nations, jealous of their rights and privileges. The Articles of Confederation which had bound them together during the fighting were a pretty flimsy League of Nations—hardly stronger than Geneva. The Articles provided that "each State retains its own sovereignty, freedom and independence."

Connecticut began to tax imports from Massachusetts at higher rates than imports from England. New York discriminated against Connecticut trade, and Connecticut retaliated by imposing a fine on citizens who traded with New York. Madison called New Jersey a "cask tapped at both ends"—the tappers being the governments of New York and Pennsylvania. He called North Carolina "a patient bleeding at both arms" between the customs restrictions of Virginia and South Carolina. The little colonial civilization was rapidly disintegrating. Money was "not worth a continental." Wars between the colonies were not improbable. Something had to be done.

To this end a few intelligent young men gathered together in Philadelphia in 1787. They wrote a constitution which created a strong central authority to bring the thirteen little states into one super-state. The central government was given sole power to regulate commerce with foreign nations, among the several states, and with the Indian tribes. The motive was to prevent the commercial destruction of one state by another. Customs duties, imposts, excise taxes, were to be uniform, with no preferences shown for Boston as against Charleston, New York as against Philadelphia. The army and navy and the power to declare war were the exclusive prerogatives of the central authority.

The opposition to this document was tremendous. Rhode Island sent no delegates to the convention at all. The vote for ratification in Massachusetts was 187 to 168; in Virginia 89 to 79; in New York 30 to 27. It was a close call. But by 1789, the required nine states had ratified, and the *United* States was born. The integration of the American continent had begun.

Integration swept westward with the purchase of the vast Louisiana territory from Napoleon, the acquiring of Florida from Spain, the war with Mexico. The Indian tribes were not only traded with, but dispossessed and often slaughtered. This minority problem was settled by the general method of Genghis Khan, a shade worse than Hitler's methods with the Jews. In recent years, a few semi-autonomous states have been set up, called Indian Reservations, as some small restitution for the rough handling of the past.

In 1860, the second great test of integration came. South Carolina demanded self-determination. Presently the other southern states echoed the demand. President Lincoln was unable to see the justice of the principle of self-determination; he called it secession. He summoned the North to bring the secessionists back into the union by force. "The federal union; it must be preserved."

If Lee had won at Gettysburg, there might now be two sovereign nations in this country. Indeed the idea of self-determination might have spread and created a dozen. Lee did not win. Lincoln won, and died as he won. He did not, like Wilson, die in vain. "One nation indivisible." This outcome was far more important than freeing the slaves. They would have been freed anyway before long. Slavery, by 1860, was no longer a paying commercial institution.

Slavery gave us another minority problem, tougher to solve than that of the Indians. It is still with us. But it is very different from minority problems in Europe. American Negroes do not desire self-determination or autonomous states. They want to be treated like human beings. To their shame, many Americans deny them this, but it will come. Our Negroes present a serious cultural problem, but they present no such military problem as do Ukrainians in Rumania or Germans in Schleswig.

The Civil War provided the second and last serious

threat to continental unity. In the late 1860's a golden spike was driven into the rail that joined the railroad line from the Atlantic to the Pacific. Fifty years later the Panama Canal clipped 10,000 miles from the ocean journey between New York and San Francisco. Cement highways, rail lines, river barges, air lines, pipe lines, power lines, postal routes, telephone wires, radio waves, now weave a gigantic web across the continent. The same language, the same money, the same form of government, the same chain store, the same movie, the same wisecrack, in Portland, Oregon, and Portland, Maine. Highbrows object to this "standardization." It is one of our greatest blessings and safeguards. If they doubt it, they had better try living in Prague or Vienna.

To say that the task of integration is complete would be premature. With 10,000,000 Americans unemployed in recent years, the task is far from complete. We share with nations the world over the recurrent crises in the breakdown of the financial system called capitalism. But at least there is little danger of any section splitting off and setting up an independent nation. We have our difficulties, but we face them under the law, not with bombs and tanks. If the people of South Dakota are not getting enough to eat, they do not have to start a "drive to the east" with armored cars and field artillery. They apply for federal relief.

In the inventory of Europe, we found acute cleavages between nations, between minorities, between religious groups, between the Mussolini brand of "fascism" and the Hitler brand. We found natural areas for trade and industry, like the watershed of the Rhine and the countries around the Mediterranean Sea, divided by armed frontiers and high tariff walls. We found that no police exist to come in when a scuffle begins and say: "Boys, that's far enough. Drop those rocks and go home!"

The inventory of the United States shows few of these tragic differences. There is a cop—the army, the militia, the local police. Citizens may talk and argue until they are black in the face—that is their right under the Constitution, and usually observed—but they may not disturb the peace by acts of violence. We have almost no economic problems arising from internal frontiers.[1] We have no warfare between religious groups to compare with the conflicts of Catholic against "Aryan," Jew against Moslem, communist against all other faiths—now found abroad. We do not need to conquer "a place in the sun" in competition with Canada, Mexico or Haiti. We have no problem of minorities in the European sense. We have had, to be sure, some comic opera skirmishes between organized communists and fascists, who used to throw rotten eggs at one another before the Red-Nazi treaties. In Spain, proponents of rival ideologies threw six-inch shells and two-ton bombs at one another. We have had bloody local labor battles and out-

[1] Since the depression, some states have put up a few barriers. California, for instance, restricts incoming migrants without property. These barriers must presently be referred to the Supreme Court.

rageous local despotisms. Now that the federal government is catching up with the Swedes in supporting the right of laborers to organize, we may expect these to decrease. The chief ideological battle in United States history has been between Republicans and Democrats. It has been going on so long that the Democrats have mislaid some of their eternal principles—like States' Rights—for the Republicans to pick up; and vice versa. This warfare is lively but hardly of military importance.

In Europe today, there are, at a conservative guess, a hundred political gas tanks either detonated or waiting for a little spark to explode them. Name one in the United States of America.

VI. THE MIGHTIEST COUNTRY

SUPPOSE Napoleon had beaten Nelson at Trafalgar and Wellington at Waterloo, and had forged a United States of Europe? A very tidy outfit it would have been, even with Russia excluded. You could put seven Texases into its two million square miles of land! It would have three hundred and eighty million people today. Lumber in the Scandinavian states, coal in the English and German states, iron in the French states, copper in the Spanish and South Slavic states, lead, zinc, mercury, sulphur, aluminum, water power in adequate quantities here and there, oil in Rumania, wheat, sugar, livestock in plenty. Four world powers—England, Germany, France, Italy—linked into one economic federation, with Sweden, Poland, Czechoslovakia, Holland, Belgium, Hungary, Yugo-Slavia, Spain, Greece, Switzerland and the rest added. One super-state, from the North Cape to Constantinople. A great capital city at Geneva. One money system. One official language. One vast power grid. Absolutely free trade throughout the country.

If Napoleon had done the task well, there would not have been a European war after his time. "Europa" and Russia might have clashed over points of honor, but hardly over raw materials. There would have been no World War, with twenty million dead; no life and death scramble for colonies, territory and trade; no hypocrisy about the "white man's burden"; no partition of Africa. "Europa," having nearly all the raw materials it required right in Europe, would have had little motive for sending traders and navies around the world, setting bad examples to business men in the United States of America.

The people of Europe would stand erect, free and strong today instead of prostrating themselves before two-by-four dictators, venting hatreds on defenseless Jews, bowed under armament expenditures which take a third and more of their taxes, and under a terrible fear which knows no surcease, day or night. Napoleon would have started the nation off with a severe dictatorship, yes. But Napoleon has been dead a long time.

Mighty as a united Europe would be, it would not be so mighty in resources as the United States is today. Of course, if Europe had been unified by Napoleon, or by anyone else, her people would undoubtedly do a better job of industrial production than is done now, so the contrast is not altogether fair. We have only a third as many citizens—130 million against 380 million—but we have half again as much land—three million square miles (not counting Alaska) against two million. In Table 1 I have prepared some comparisons between the United States, Europe and the Soviet Union. They will repay a little study.[1]

The figures in the table are all percentages of world totals, to show the share of each continental group. Let

[1] An explanation of how tables 1, 2 and 3 were prepared will be found in the Appendix.

TABLE 1

APPROXIMATE PER CENT OF WORLD TOTAL

(in recent years)

	CONTINENTAL UNITED STATES	EUROPE WITHOUT RUSSIA	RUSSIA
General			
Population (number)	6%	19%	9%
Land area (sq. miles)	6	4	16
Arable land (sq. miles)	3	4	5
Tons of RR freight (ton-miles)	43	16	28
Railroad mileage (miles)	34	26	7
Telephones installed (no.)	50	34	3
Industrial raw material production ($–1928)	39	18	5
Food and Fiber production ($–1928)	14	22	8
Energy Production			
Total horsepower generated	50	..	..
Horsepower without motor vehicles	42	34	..
Electric power produced (kwh)	35	35	8
Coal produced (tons)	34	45	9
Petroleum produced (tons)	62	3	10
Natural gas (cubic meters)	90	4	2
Mineral Production			
Iron ore (tons)	29	44	16
Copper ore (tons)	32	8	5
Lead (tons)	22	19	3
Zinc (tons)	30	25	4
Natural phosphate (tons)	28	9	29
Potash	8	83	8
Sulphur (tons)	78	13	0
Steel production (tons)	38	41	13
Pig iron production (tons)	36	43	14

Food and Fiber Production	CONTINENTAL UNITED STATES	EUROPE WITHOUT RUSSIA	RUSSIA
Cereals (wheat, corn, rye, barley, oats) ($—1928)	27%	34%	..%
Wheat (quintals)	16	34	20
Corn (quintals)	53	16	4
Sugar (quintals)	6	23	9
Cotton (quintals)	50	1	10
Wool (tons)	12	15	5
Wood pulp (tons)	24	50	3
Manufactures			
Automobiles (no.)	79	19	0.4
Buses and trucks (no.)	66	16	13
Cotton goods ($)	30	..	..
Silk goods ($)	67	..	..
Rubber goods ($)	67	..	..
Chemicals ($)	43	..	..
Movie films ($)	90	..	..

NOTE: See appendix, pages 189-190 for sources of the figures given in these tables.

us first run down the share of the United States, and fix our place in world economy. It is almost unbelievable until you see the cold percentages. We have about 6 per cent of the population of the world, and about 6 per cent of the land area—not counting Alaska. Keep that figure *6* in mind as you study the ratios. When the figure is greater than 6, it means that we have *more* than our world share would be on a per capita basis.

We move 43 per cent of the world's freight, produce nearly 40 per cent of the world's raw materials for industry, generate half the world's horsepower and 35 per cent of its electric power. We produce 34 per cent of the coal, 62 per cent of the petroleum. We are strong in the "big four" metals—iron ore, copper, lead, zinc. We make more than a third of the world's pig iron and steel. Incidentally, we have thirty huge mills for the new continuous process of making steel sheet and strip. No other nation has more than one.

We grow half the world's corn. We have half the world's telephones. In New York City alone there are more telephones than in Russia, India, China and Poland combined. We have four-fifths of the world's automobiles, two-thirds of the trucks and buses, more than half the radio sets.[1] We consume two-thirds of the world's rubber and silk goods, produce 90 per cent of the world's moving pictures.

[1] We have 38 million radio sets, Germany comes next with 10 million, then Great Britain with 8.5 million, France 4.2 million, Russia 3.8 million, Japan 3.4 million. Figures from Federal Communications Commission, 1938.

Comparing our economy with that of Europe (outside of Russia), and with Russia, we find many significant figures. In the ratios given in Table 1, we lead or tie in twenty-one items, Europe leads or ties in fourteen items, Russia in only three. Both Europe and Russia have more arable land than we have, but we are far out in front in the production of energy and in industrial raw materials. Europe leads both the United States and Russia in food and fiber production. This is natural, because she has so many more people to feed. To grow food on the land, you must feed the crops themselves certain substances, including potash. Europe has a big lead in the production of potash, but recently we have discovered deposits of one hundred million tons in New Mexico, most of it on government land. We need not worry about this mineral. Russia has large unworked deposits of various raw materials, especially in Siberia, but it is evident that Russia has a long pull ahead before her people can enter the industrial class of the other two continental groups.

The tremendous thing about the table is the fact that the United States, one nation, is more powerful industrially than Great Britain, France, Germany, Italy combined, with twenty other nations thrown in for good measure! European countries may have the cannon fodder, but they cannot make the cannon as well as we can. The figures clearly indicate that a unified Europe would be a powerful combination, close to self-sufficiency in its industrial equipment. But when a third of its manpower goes into the trenches, it must rapidly disintegrate as an operating economy.

Now let us turn to Table 2. Here we find another series of dramatic contrasts. The United States is compared with five Great Powers—Great Britain (not including the Empire), Germany (as of 1937), France, Italy (not including Albania), Japan. *Of the twenty-five ratios listed, the United States leads in everything but the production of potash, sugar and silk!* Look at the fat, massed figures in the United States column, and the thin, scattered ratios, the many zeros, in the other columns. Look at the pitiful ratios for arable land, for freight tonnage, for electric power, motor vehicles, copper, lead, phosphates, wheat, corn, cotton. These Great Powers are living skeletons compared to the United States.

Germany's gains through her recent conquests are hard to calculate precisely. The status of the protectorates is ambiguous; boundaries, area, and ownership of resources continue to shift. I have gone down the German column in this table, adding figures for Austria and all of Czechoslovakia, and have found the increases less than I should have expected.

Twelve items register no gain at all; thirteen—including land and population—rise from a tenth of one per cent to as much as 3 per cent. A tenth of one per cent of the arable land of the world is of course a gain of more than 10 per cent to Germany's total. The largest

TABLE 2

APPROXIMATE PER CENT OF WORLD TOTALS

	U. S.	GRT. BRITAIN	GERMANY	FRANCE	ITALY	JAPAN
General						
Population	6%	2%	3%	2%	2%	3%
Land area	6	0.2	0.4	0.4	0.2	0.3
Arable land	3	0.3	0.6	0.4	0.4	0.2
Tons of RR freight hauled	43	3	6	3	1	1
Railroad mileage	34	3	5	4	2	2
Motor vehicles produced	76	8	5	3	1	*
Energy Production						
Electric power produced	35	7	11	4	4	6
Coal produced	34	19	14	3	1	3
Petroleum produced	62	0	*	*	*	*
Mineral Production						
Iron ore	29	8	4	19	*	*
Copper	32	0	2	0	*	5
Lead	22	2	5	0	2	1
Zinc	30	*	9	0	4	1
Natural phosphate	28	0	0	*	0	1
Potash	8	0	63	16	0	*
Sulphur	78	0	0	0	13	8
Steel production	38	10	15	6	2	4
Pig iron production	36	8	15	8	1	2
Foods and Fibers						
Wheat	16	1	4	6	5	1
Corn	53	0	0	*	3	0
Sugar	6	2	7	3	1	1
Cotton	50	0	0	0	*	0
Wool	12	3	1	1	1	0
Silk	0	0	0	1	3	80
Wood pulp	24	1	11	2	1	19

* less than half of 1%

increases occur in woodpulp (from 11 to 14%) and sugar (from 7 to 10%). Iron ore and wheat both go from 4 to 5 per cent of world totals. Iron has been a serious shortage for Germany, and wheat has been short; the new wheat will come mostly from Slovakia.

The fact is that there is no comparison between the United States and any one of the other Great Powers. It is unfair to line up with them. From the industrial point of view, we are so far ahead that we could take on all five of them, with Russia thrown in. If the whole shooting match should combine to attack us, we clearly have the industrial capacity to stand them off.

A comparison of the United States with the British Empire would be less one-sided. Here are some figures covering an average of production in the years 1930 and 1933, prepared by John C. de Wilde for the Foreign Policy Association:

Per cent of world total	*United States per cent*	*British Empire per cent*
Petroleum	63	2
Coal	37	23
Iron ore	27	11
Copper	28	20
Lead	26	37
Zinc	32	27
Tin	0	43
Bauxite	18	7
Rubber	0	65
Cotton	52	18
Wool	12	49

The material output of the British Empire, including as it does Canada, Australia, New Zealand, South Africa, India, Egypt, the East Indies and many other areas, makes an impressive statistical total. But it is very vulnerable to attack, with tenuous lifelines all over the planet. Of the eleven items listed, the United States leads in seven.

I have also collected figures on South America, Africa and Australia as continental economic units. They are not worth presenting. No one of these continents is a potential rival, for many years at least, to the United States, Europe or Russia. South America and Africa will always be handicapped by having their broadest areas in the tropics. Australia is handicapped by having only 21 million acres of arable land—where the United States has more than 400 million. The interior of Australia is largely desert.

Now let us make a few comparisons from the point of view of resources. Heretofore we have been talking mostly of production. Production will fizzle out unless there is ore in the ground, timber on the hills. Table 3 gives some light on this question. It is a solid table, with many symbols, but it may be summarized as follows:

The United States is well equipped with most resources, especially arable land, coal, waterpower, sulphur. It is short of mercury, and far short of tin, nickel, manganese and chromite. It raises no rubber or coffee.

If North America is taken as a unit, the inventory is

TABLE 3

EXTENT OF KNOWN NATURAL RESOURCES

	U. S.	N. AM.	WEST. HEMIS.	EUROPE	RUSSIA	GREAT BRITAIN	GERMANY	FRANCE	ITALY	JAPAN
Arable land	++	++	++	—	++	—	—	—	—	—
Waterpower	++	++	++	+	+	——	—	—	+	—
Coal	++	++	++	++	+	+	++	—	——	—
Petroleum	+	+	++	—	+	o	——	——	——	——
Iron	+	++	++	+	—	+	—	++	——	——
Copper	+	++	++	+	—*	o	—	o	——	—
Lead	+	++	++	+	—*	—	—	——	—	——
Zinc	+	++	++	+	—*	——	+	——	+	——
Aluminum clays	+	+	++	++	—*	o	—	++	+	o
Tin	——	—	+	—	—*	—	——	o	o	——
Nickel	——	++	++	——	—*	o	o	o	o	o
Manganese	——	—	—*	—	++	o	+	o	o	o
Chromite	——	—	—*	++	++	o	o	o	o	+
Tungsten	+	+	++	+	—*	——	o	o	o	——
Mercury	—	+	+	++	—*	o	——	o	++	——
Phosphate	+	+	+	—	++	o	o	——	o	——
Potash	+	+	+	++	—*	o	++	+	o	——
Sulphur	++	++	++	+	—*	o	o	o	++	+
Timber	+	++	++	+	++	—	—	—	——	—
Natural rubber	o	——	—*	o	o	o	o	o	o	o
Cereals	++	++	++	+	++	—	—	+	+	—
Sugar	—	++	++	+	+	——	+	—	——	——
Coffee	o	—	++	o	o	o	o	o	o	o

KEY

++ Surplus — Shortage o None

—— Way short * Can be developed

even stronger. Manganese and chromite are still short, but supplies exist and could be further developed—especially in Cuba.

If the Western Hemisphere is taken as a unit, rubber is the only major shortage. Brazil, where rubber was first found, still grows some and could produce enough for the West, given capital and improved technical methods. Bolivian tin may or may not be adequate for all Western needs.

Comparing the United States with Europe, resources are perhaps a little stronger on our side, but not by very much. Europe is short of arable land per capita, short of petroleum, tin, nickel, manganese, phosphates, and of course coffee and rubber.

Russian resources as they stand are weaker than those of the United States and Europe, but many of the mineral shortages can be made up. Production from some of the vast deposits in the Urals and Siberia already shows spectacular acceleration.[1] In a few more years, the Russian resource inventory may rival that of Europe. In arable land, timber, petroleum, manganese, phosphates, cereals, it is already stronger than Europe's inventory.

Comparing the resources of the United States with those of the five Great Powers, one by one—Great Britain, Germany, France, Italy, Japan—we find a condition similar to that noted earlier in current production. There is no real comparison. The shortages of the great powers

[1] For a first-hand description of Russian resources, see *In Search of Soviet Gold*, by an American mining engineer, John D. Littlepage.

are pathetic. Germany, for instance, out of the twenty-three materials listed, shows "nothing" in seven, "way short" in three, "short" in eight. Her resource budget is out of the red in only five materials. She has substantial surpluses in coal and potash alone. With Austria she gained a little iron and waterpower, a trace of petroleum, and seven million people to feed.

Great Britain, France, Italy and Japan are in still sorrier condition. We must remember, however, that as technology advances and substitutes are found, the resource inventory changes. My table is made with reference to industrial demands today. In 1960 the picture may be different.

MAN AND LAND

It has been estimated by E. M. East and others that under current agricultural practice, a nation needs 2.5 acres of arable land for every man, woman and child in the population, to produce enough food and fiber crops for a high living standard. On this assumption, only half a dozen countries in the world are over the top. Here they are, in arable acres per capita:

Canada	28.9
Argentina	18.5
New Zealand	12.2
Russia	4.2
United States	3.3
Australia	3.2

Most other countries are under the 2.5 line. The list goes on:

Europe—17 nations	1.3
Denmark—best in Europe	2.2
Greece—worst in Europe	.5+
England and Wales	.6
Germany	1.1
France	1.3
Italy	1.3
Japan (worst on record)	.5
China (probably a pretty wild estimate)	.8
India (ditto)	.7

The figures are from Dr. O. W. Willcox's book *Nations Can Live at Home*, about which we have more to say in the next section. Canada looks too high to me. The arable land may be there, but also a short growing season, and billions of mosquitoes. I doubt if lands in the Northwest Territory, however rich, will ever be extensively colonized. Australia has approximately the same ratio as the United States. We have 130 million people; Australia less than 7 million. Another million or so of settlers would throw Australia under the 2.5 line. We could accommodate 35 million more people before crossing the line. (But if we do not check water and wind erosion, this statistical conclusion may change rapidly in the wrong direction.)

The United States is two and a half times better off than Europe in its man-land ratio, a further score for resource strength and self-sufficiency. It is not, however, so strong as Russia. Argentina and New Zealand have vast land surpluses—but some of the Argentine acreage, like that of Canada, may be too cold for comfort. Patagonia has many of the characteristics of the country around the Great Slave Lake. As in the earlier tables, the other Great Powers are again short of resources. Japan, with only half an acre per head, is worst of all.

Almost any way you look at it, from the economic point of view the United States is far, far in the lead. Russia, the other great continental nation, still trails to the rear. Behind Russia, in resource strength if not in production, trail the Great Powers—England, Germany, France, Italy, Japan. Bundle all six of them together, and we can match their resources. We could more than hold our own against the British Empire itself. In event of war, we have oil in a dozen home states. England must send ships down the Bay of Biscay, past submarines, airplanes, mines, in the Mediterranean, to pipe lines in the Near East—3,000 miles to reach the nearest oil supply.

We are mightier than the other powers because we are a different kind of nation altogether. We have no more reason for crowing over Germany than we have for crowing over Texas. I have said this before, and I propose to go right on saying it. Peace or war in the next year or two may depend upon enough American citizens and voters getting this idea of integration firmly planted in their minds. We are stronger, never forget, not because we are so smart, but because we were fortunate enough to land in the most impregnable geographical area on earth. We then had sense enough to keep it unified.

When President Jefferson bought Louisiana from Napoleon in 1803, Napoleon said: "This enlargement of its territory consolidates the power of the United States for all time. Perhaps people will reproach me because in two or three centuries the Americans become too powerful for Europe." The prophecy was shrewd but conservative. It did not take two or three centuries. It took one hundred and twenty years.

VII. CAN THE UNITED STATES BE SELF-SUFFICIENT?

SUPPOSE some genie suddenly threw an electrified fence around the United States charged with such terrific voltage that goods could neither come in nor go out, not even in airplanes. How much would the people of America be handicapped?

If it were done tomorrow, we should be very severely handicapped. If the genie gave due notice that the current would not be turned on until January 1, 1942, the shock could be greatly lessened. Now, or three years later, we should have the materials for plenty to eat, plenty to wear, plenty of houses to live in. Food, clothing and shelter could not be shut out. But if the fence went around Great Britain, perhaps half the population would presently be starving. If it went around Germany, France, Italy or Japan, there would be serious hunger, and a complete breakdown of industrial production for lack of raw materials.

Here are the current major shortages in the United States as listed by the War Department. In event of war, steps would have to be taken to insure the supply, or to develop substitutes:

Rubber	Tin	Shellac
Silk	Antimony	Wool
Jute and sisal	Mercury	Hides

Sugar	Coco shells	Opium and a few other drugs
Manganese	Coffee	
Chromium	Camphor	Mica
Nickel	Tungsten	Nitrates

By way of a check, here are the ten major imports into the United States in 1935. Each was valued at fifty million dollars or more. The list is given in order of dollar value:

1. Coffee
2. Cane sugar
3. Crude rubber
4. Raw silk
5. Newsprint
6. Vegetable oils
7. Tin
8. Chemicals and drugs
9. Fruits and nuts
10. Furs

We paid for these imports primarily with the following ten products:

1. Cotton
2. Tobacco
3. Petroleum
4. Fruits and nuts
5. Automobile parts
6. Copper
7. Meats and fats
8. Industrial machinery
9. Boards and planks
10. Furs

Observe the whimsies of foreign trade, where we pay for furs with furs, and nuts with nuts. The incoming furs are mostly dressed; the outgoing, undressed. The fine distinction in nuts I have not run to earth, and do not intend to.

The War Department's shortages can be classified into three divisions: (1) Those that come from Canada, Mexico, the Caribbean, and that will keep right on coming, unless the War Department is far less efficient than we like to believe; (2) Those that can be compensated for by stimulating home production; (3) Those that come from South America—not including Colombia and Venezuela which border on the Caribbean—and from abroad. Group 3 is the difficult one. Let us briefly consider each group.

1. From North America and the Caribbean we can get sisal (Yucatan), sugar (Cuba), some coffee, some drugs, some chromium, antimony, tungsten, manganese, plenty of nickel (Canada), coco shells.

2. We can stimulate home production in our deposits of manganese, antimony, mercury, tungsten, mica, although the costs may be higher than for imported ore. Where our deposits are small, we can practice thrift. We can readily grow more beet sugar, wool, hides. We have a great government plant at Muscle Shoals in "standby" condition, ready to produce nitrates from the air when the President gives the word. Air and power are the only raw materials needed. There happens to be plenty of opium now in storage, seized by the Narcotics Division. Poppies can also be grown.

3. The chief problems remaining are thus rubber, silk, coffee, tin. Rubber is grown in Brazil, but most of our supply comes from the East Indies. If this shipping line were cut, we should be in a serious condition. Two things might be done: stimulate Brazilian plantations (Secretary Wallace has a plan for this, but production

would take some years); put "Duprene," a synthetic rubber, into mass production. We will touch on this point later.

The nearest considerable tin supply in the West is in Bolivia. If this were cut off, we should be in another jam. No more tin cans. Modern civilization, if I may say so, practically rests on tin cans and rubber tires. At a pinch, however, we could pack our soup and condensed milk in aluminum cans, or use some other alloy to coat the iron—of which "tin" cans are chiefly composed.

Coffee is grown in Mexico, Central America and the West Indies, but the chief source is Brazil. If Brazil were out, coffee cultivation could be increased around the Caribbean, but it would take time. We confirmed addicts might suffer for a while. Only one cup for breakfast.

Silk was a real problem until just the other day. Rayon stockings do not please the ladies; powder charges for big guns must be wrapped in silk bags. The problem has now been solved by a synthetic fiber shortly to be manufactured in large quantities. We will return to this point also in a moment.

In case of war, with Canadian nickel and other minerals still available; with the Caribbean Sea kept open by the navy; and with some fast work on the home front—can you recall the Food Administration in 1917? —only tin, manganese, and raw rubber would be really difficult. The government has been laying in reserve supplies of these materials.

In the case of the electrified fence, with the rest of North America blocked off, the shortages would be more serious. Research men would have to go to work on substitutes for ferrous alloys, chromite, nickel, manganese; on rubber and jute substitutes; on drugs. Beet sugar growers, wool growers, producers of hides, would become part of the national defense. A little coffee might be grown in California. No more bananas. Some of those nuts would fall by the wayside. Most of our factories, however, could continue to operate. Many new factories would go into action, manufacturing substitutes. We should be pinched, here and there, but nobody need go hungry. We could carry on.

But such a fence would crucify the people of any other industrial nation on earth, except Russia.

There are no imports from Europe which are absolutely vital for our well-being. No important industries are as dependent upon European imports as they were at the outbreak of the World War. If these imports were shut off, the chief sufferers would be traders whose interest is vested in the import business, and consumers of such luxuries as French lace and English leather goods. If we had to, we could compensate the traders and deprive ourselves of the luxuries. "The United States alone," says *Plan Age*, "possesses the geographic isolation and resources to complement a determination to avoid war."

MARCH OF THE INVENTORS

This brings us to a very interesting line of thought. If the United States is close to self-sufficiency today, needing only a few substitutes to make it theoretically complete, why cannot smaller areas, by developing bigger and better substitutes, become self-sufficient tomorrow? If they can do so, why need their people go out with blood in their eye, looking for raw materials?

Dr. Willcox demonstrates that the old rule of 2.5 acres of arable land per head of population, for self-sufficiency, is becoming obsolete. The new science of agrobiology is driving the ratio down. The agrobiologists have found the *limit* of plant vitality, and "this limit is vastly higher than the best that traditional methods could ever promise." In favored circumstances, a quarter of an acre would turn the trick!

A poison-free, moist soil which contains more than eight units of each of the indispensable plant foods will produce the maximum yield of any plant that grows, whether pansies or pine trees. Water must be controlled to give supplementary irrigation in the growing season, plant food (fertilizers) must be regulated by the new formulas, and yields can be produced—and are now in fact being produced—which stagger the imagination. The theoretical maximum for corn is 225 bushels to the acre. It has actually been grown. The cheapest source of food energy for human beings is sugar cane. "A perultra sugar cane with .33 per cent of nitrogen can produce the complete minimum ration for a population of 69,600 to the square mile." The densest populations now known are 2,000 to the square mile of arable land. We should not be very happy eating nothing but sugar cane and its derivatives, but at least we need not starve. The calculation is purely theoretical, of course, to show what could be done.

Take England, says Dr. Willcox. For the expenditure of 150 million a year, about half the annual cost of the navy, England could remodel her 32 million acres of arable land on agrobiological principles, and render her people completely self-sufficient in bread, oatmeal, potatoes, sugar, beef, milk, eggs, pork, mutton and poultry. The terror of blockade and starvation could be eliminated. In five years, subsistence could be reached; in ten years, comfort; and in fifteen years, luxury in the food supply. But to do this the English must have supplies of fertilizers.

Take Germany. When the Reich was founded in 1870, the population fed itself on home soil. After unification came expansion in manufacturing and trade. Population grew rapidly in those days. Presently the home food supply became inadequate, and export outlets had to be found to exchange manufactured goods for imports of wheat and beef. After the turn of the century, according to Dr. Willcox, industrial leaders notified the Kaiser that foreign markets for manufactured goods were narrowing, as backward nations built their own factories, that good colonies were scarce, that the Americas were protected by the Monroe Doctrine, and that the only feasible course was to challenge the British Empire. A great navy should be built and aggressive trade policies pushed forward. Only so could the German population be fed and held secure. The Kaiser accepted the logic, and the World War was the result. England could not tolerate a great navy threatening *her* food supply.

In 1934, Germany was 25 per cent short in the home food supply, and short in fiber crops. As matters stood, the country "seemingly cannot avoid sinking to a lower level of existence unless the wall that encloses it melts away, or is blown up." Hitler is now busy blowing it up. But there were really two choices: Either hack a way out with the sword, or remove the fear of shortage by agrobiology. Germany could do a better job at this than England. She could readily grow all her foodstuffs, much of her fibers. She could grow potatoes to feed to hogs to insure her desperately needed fats. In 1900, of course, such a program was impossible. Agrobiology had not been heard from then.

Take Japan. As we saw earlier, Japan's ratio of population to arable land is the worst on earth. Japan has almost no domestic animals, for there is not enough land to feed them on. The permanent food deficit is 10 to 15 per cent, despite the universal and dreary diet of rice and fish. The islands are way short of wool, cotton, hemp, vegetable fibers, oilseed. They have few minerals; very little salt, petroleum, timber; no rubber. Their major raw materials suitable for export are coal, cement and silk. These cannot give enough exchange value to feed her people. So raw materials are imported in vast quantities, manufactured at very low money costs, and re-exported as cotton cloth, toys, electric fixtures, and all the other commodities that have lately been deluging world markets, stamped "Made in Japan."

In 1860, Japan had 30 million people, was completely self-contained, easy-going and reasonably happy. Her 70 million people are not happy today. It has taken three short generations to work out to the end of the limb. Population must now be exported, or export industries must be developed to supply the home population. The people do not want to move, so the exports must. This is a very ticklish balance, with world markets in the condition they are today. Certainly one reason why the Japanese have so ruthlessly invaded China is the attempt to find an export market they can count on. "The pressure of the Japanese population is now the most dynamic on the face of the earth." Peoples will always fight for their material survival.

All this does not daunt Dr. Willcox. He proceeds to demonstrate how the Japanese, by exerting a little of their famous discipline and ingenuity, could present themselves with the equivalent of 47 million acres of new farm land, insure self-sufficiency, and double their present food standards!

Agrobiology is applicable not only to food but to fiber crops, drug crops, timber crops, to everything that grows. A gasoline substitute can be made from wood—16 pounds of wood waste to the gallon. It is already being used in Europe for buses and trucks. Engines can run on alcohol. The cheapest source of alcohol is cane sugar. A crop of ten tons of sugar to the acre is the equivalent of 2,500 gallons of gasoline. Agrobiologists could grow enough cane sugar on an area half the size of Maryland to run all the motor vehicles in the United States. Alcohol is not so good a fuel as gasoline, gallon for gallon, but it will operate cars. Out in Kansas they are making *Agrol*, a power alcohol, from surplus corn. Farmers mix it with regular gasoline.

In 1926, Professor H. E. Woodman developed a famous method for shortening the protein cycle, thus speeding up the food supply. It has long been known that young plants contain relatively more protein than mature plants. They absorb their nitrogen early. Good. Let us now harvest crops when they are half grown, and get better than half the protein yield. Sow another crop and harvest again before cold weather comes. People cannot eat half-grown alfalfa or corn, but cattle can. "When this easy method of obtaining abundant supplies of concentrated stock feed comes to be generally adopted, a steer can be raised on the crop of half an acre, and beef, eggs, butter and milk, now relatively the most expensive of all foods, should become even cheaper than bread." Wool should become as cheap as cotton.

Speaking of wool, a substitute is now being made of skimmed milk. "Cheddar" cheese can now be made anywhere by proper selection of bacteria. Radio-active sodium, used in hospitals, is being made from ordinary salt. Aluminum is one of the most common elements in the crust of the planet. It occurs in clays, of which one, bauxite, is chiefly used to make the metal. The research men are now finding cheaper methods to make it from any aluminum clay. Every sizeable nation has deposits. Magnesium and phosphorus can be recovered from sea water, though this is still far from being a practical industrial operation. Pigs can be fed from the disintegration products of wood pulp. Tomato plants can be grown fifteen feet tall, by tray agriculture. Sugar can be made from waste vegetable matter by the agency of bacteria.

Germany is making rope from cellulose, candy from woodchips, rubber from coal and lime. Iron pipes are being replaced for some uses by pipes made of glass. Materials for glass are common everywhere. A fabric is now being made from spun glass. The synthetic "Bakelite" finds many uses as a plastic. When Japanese electric light bulbs invaded American markets, the General Electric Company proceeded to invent bulb-making machinery so efficient that it could cut under the price of the Japanese product. This is a safer method than abandoning the trade to the vagaries of 5,000 miles of ocean travel. The President of the International Nickel Company recently remarked: "If nickel should become less available to the steel maker, he would promptly, through metallurgical research, find substitutes." Chemists have largely replaced dye stuffs from plants and animals, with dyes from coal tar. Mr. Ford makes steering wheels out of soy beans.

One of our major imports, we noted earlier, was newsprint manufactured from wood pulp. This trade is headed for eclipse. A southern chemist, Dr. C. H. Herty, after years of research perfected a method for making newsprint and other types of paper from fast-growing southern pine. He found out how to eliminate the pitch, which heretofore has made this wood impractical for paper. A dozen great mills are now being built in the southern states. The good effects are twofold: More self-sufficiency for the nation; more cash income for southern industrial workers and farmers. The United States Forest Service is co-operating with a conservation program, teaching farmers how to crop their woodlots so that the supply may never run out.

Father Nieuwland, a Catholic priest and scientist, has developed an artificial rubber. Du Pont took over his patents and christened the product "Duprene." It is said that if the demand became great enough, Duprene could be turned out by mass production methods for 25 cents a pound. Natural rubber has sold from 15 cents to $1 a pound in recent years. The artificial product is more durable than natural rubber, for some uses.

Perhaps the most exciting new invention in self-sufficiency is that announced simultaneously in the fall of 1938 by du Pont and the Celanese Corporation of America. Both are building new eight million dollar plants to manufacture synthetic silk—not rayon, *silk*. Both are expected to be in production before the end of 1939. It is one of those common cases of simultaneous invention. Rayon has taken many markets away from the industrious silkworm, but it has proven too lustrous, too inelastic, and not sufficiently sheer to flatter ladies' ankles. Both the new synthetic yarns promise to give them stockings form-fitted, stronger, more sheer, and cheaper than anything before known. One of the products is made, it is said, from air, water and coal. Of 100 million dollars' worth of raw silk imported annually, 75 million is used in hosiery. That trade now goes glimmering. Japanese exporters are in a panic, but they are not finding the rest of us very sympathetic.

These new substitutes are not random inventions. *They are part of an inevitable scientific trend.* Scientists have discovered the fundamental bricks out of which the material universe is constructed. They know many of the laws which govern the behavior of electrons, atoms, molecules. They are beginning to take these fundamental bricks and build up a desired material. Some day they may be able to construct *any* desired material, organic or inorganic. The only requirements will be plenty of cheap electric power and some air, water, coal, wood waste, corn shucks. This will not happen tomorrow, but when it comes, no people need ever again march out with blood in their eye, looking for raw materials. I have often discussed the trend of invention in other writings, with especial reference to internal problems. It is interesting to see how it will have a vital effect on international problems.

Substitute and synthetic materials, if they fill the bill, not only increase self-sufficiency, but ease the drain on natural resources which are getting low. Thus by using southern pitch pine for paper, we can hold the watersheds of our northern rivers against the destruction of forest cover for pulpwood. By using aluminum, which is abundant, we can husband copper reserves. By using a percentage of alcohol from corn or sugar in our motors, we can save petroleum, which is especially valuable for lubricating purposes. Speaking of conservation, Dr. Harcourt Morgan of the TVA has calculated that we have just about enough phosphate rock to maintain our soils at par. To export it, as we are now doing, he says, is a crime against the land, grasses and forests of America.

In the first flush of the industrial revolution, with steamships and railroads girdling the globe, it was natural enough to think that more invention meant more economic interdependence. It was true for a time. It is no longer true. "It is too bad," says Lancelot Hogben, "that those who have the will to peace too often resist propaganda for self-sufficiency with arguments which antedate the synthetic manufacture of nitrate fertilizers."

VIII. TWENTY MILLION GRAND

PERHAPS most people who have studied the situation with any care would admit that the people of the United States could live fairly comfortably on their own natural resources if they had to. If Canada, Mexico and Cuba were included in the orbit of exchange, it would be easier, and with South America, easier still. From the point of view of adequate resources to operate a power civilization, the New World, by making a few adjustments, need ask no favors from the Old World. The promotion of a rubber crop in Brazil would be the most difficult adjustment.

This situation is all very well as an engineering matter. But other students point out that it is dollars which make the world go round. A powerful group of business men in this country, supported by many professors, maintains that foreign trade, even if not absolutely necessary in a dire emergency, is the only road to real prosperity. They say we cannot sell all our goods at home, so we must sell them abroad. They say we should stimulate exports, loan capital to foreign countries, encourage a vigorous exchange between nation and nation. They say the prosperity of American farmers depends on selling abroad their surpluses of cotton, wheat, tobacco. Then they point a moral. Isn't it better, they say, for each nation to produce the things it can make best, and exchange them for the things which other nations can make best? This leads to international economy, efficiency and good will. It leads, they say, to peace.

Does it? The last world war broke out when international trading was at a peak. One of the reasons why it broke out was the energy with which German business men, aided by the Kaiser, were going after the markets of English business men.

If the governments of the various nations got together and figured out what surplus raw materials and manufactured goods their citizens could readily spare, and then, through a world clearing house, arranged a gigantic international swap, plugging shortages with surpluses, we probably should have an exchange system which made for efficiency and peace.

But that is not the way it is now done. Far from it. For a time, during the war, the Allies had a supreme economic council which arranged something like it for half the world. But it was dropped when the war ended. Most "nations" do not swap surpluses, and never have. Private citizens and corporations within each nation do the bulk of the foreign trading. Russia, Germany and Italy in recent years trade through one government agency controlling exports and imports, but it is a great innovation and is held by many to be reprehensible. Private citizens engaging in foreign trade think first of the number of dollars, pounds or francs they can make out of it. Almost the last thing they think about is whether the people of the nation really need the goods they are importing, or whether the people of the other nation really need the goods they are exporting. Can the goods be sold at a profit?

If traders can persuade Chinese to use obsolete motor horns on rickshaws, or Mongolians to enhance their prestige by wearing four hats, one on top of the other, or tropical islanders to buy sleigh-bells by the hundred dozen, they feel that the wheels of commerce are being lubricated and that they are rendering a patriotic service to their country.

Governments help business men, as we shall see, but the happy picture of the several "nations" giving of their riches to one another in friendly exchange is unadulterated moonshine. Look at the bitter complaints which go up when Russia suddenly invades the world market to "dump" [1] wheat. Look at South America before the war started, with business men from England, Germany, Japan, France, Italy, Holland and the United States, at each other's throats, often trying to sell the same things—electric machinery, boots and shoes, automobiles. What kind of peaceful swapping do you call this? We are going to get all tangled up in our search for facts if we think of "nations" exchanging their products. Business men do most of the exchanging, and their motive is a cash return.

[1] *Dumping* is selling goods abroad at lower prices than they can be bought for at home; often selling them below what it costs to produce them at home.

In the early years of the Republic, American citizens engaged heavily in foreign trade. At that time we lived along the Atlantic coast, and the West was an unexplored wilderness. By 1807 a million tons of shipping flew the American flag. War between France and England promptly got these ships into trouble. They were captured at sea for violating British rules. American sailors were impressed, and forced to serve in the British navy. Napoleon seized ten million dollars' worth of our ships and cargoes. President Jefferson, like President Wilson a century later, tried to avoid war. An embargo law was passed by Congress, forbidding American merchantmen to sail for foreign ports. New England shipping interests roared their disapproval; they were making fortunes on the ships which did get through the French and British lines. The embargo was repealed in 1809. Seizures continued.

In 1812 we declared war on England, in part because of this interference with our trade. The war did not solve the difficulty, or give us "freedom of the seas." It did, however, turn our eyes inward to our home markets, and to the possibility of developing factories in America. Statesmen were alarmed at the dangers of too much dependence on a foreign trade which could so easily be interrupted, which could so easily lead to war. That alarm is still with us.

For a long time, though foreign trade expanded, our major energies went into developing the North American continent. One huge slice after another was added to our domain—the Louisiana purchase in 1803, 900,000 square miles bought from Napoleon for twenty-seven million dollars; Florida, ceded by Spain in 1819; Texas in 1845; the Oregon Territory ("fifty-four forty or fight") in 1846; and all the rest of the Southwest soon after. We took the latter from Mexico after defeating her in a fight over Texas, and paid her fifteen millions for it. Alaska we bought from Russia in 1867, for 7.2 millions—600,000 square miles. That rounded out our continental empire.

In 1898 we defeated Spain in an inglorious war, and took over Puerto Rico, the Philippines and the guardianship of Cuba. Thereupon we began to imitate other great empires which were busy annexing colonies, exploiting native workers, and carrying the white man's burden. "Dollar diplomacy" was a nickname which stuck to this campaign. American bankers went into Cuba, Haiti, the Dominican Republic, Panama, Nicaragua, Liberia and China. Presently the marines went after them. The flag follows trade. It was all very spirited. Theodore Roosevelt waved the big stick, and stirred up a revolution in Panama in order to get a right of way for the Canal. The martyred McKinley, after subduing the Philippine patriots, enunciated the spirit of the times. Our rule, he said, was inspired by the desire "to educate the Filipinos and uplift and civilize and Christianize them, and by God's grace do the very best we can by them, as our fellowmen for whom Christ also died."

Lofty sentiments like these are frequently mixed with foreign trade. Cortez and Pizarro exchanged Christianity for gold in their own quaint way. Four centuries later, the government of the United States forsook its internal task and became a co-laborer in the vineyard with England, France, Germany, Italy, Russia and Japan. These governments tried to seize every patch of the planet not nailed down. They divided up Africa, chipped the edges off China. Business men did the trading, but governments furnished the gunboats and the marines. Statesmen banged the rostrum to tell of the glory of new places in the sun.

Despite the insular possessions and the glory, the United States found its farm exports declining from 1900 to 1914. Then the war turned trading and traders upside down. The subject is complex and full of technicalities about foreign currencies, tariff schedules, export subsidies, international gold standards. Let us try to see what foreign trade really means, in correct proportions and in simple terms.

A BALANCE SHEET OF FOREIGN TRADE

In 1934, Mr. George N. Peek, special adviser on foreign trade, prepared a table for President Roosevelt. It summarized all the financial transactions of Americans with people in the world outside the United States, for the twenty years from 1914 through 1933. Nothing like it was ever prepared before. It took months to compile, and yet was so simple that every literate citizen could at last understand what foreign trade means, and how it works. I will reproduce the table in round billions.

From 1914 through 1933

Americans sold goods to the outside world valued at about	90	(billions)
They bought goods from the outside world valued at	62	
Leaving the world in their debt	28	
The world owed them for interest, freight, and other charges	11	
Gross total owed to Americans in 20 years	39	
Against which the outside world paid Americans in gold	2	
And charged Americans for entertainment of tourists, for remittances sent abroad by immigrants, etc.	13	
Total offsets to bill	15	
Leaving the world in debt to Americans for 20 years' business	24	(billions)

This debt was represented by:

War debts due from foreign governments to the government of the United States	10	
Increase in loans and investments abroad by American citizens and corporations	14	
Total as above	24	(billions)

Here is the whole story. At the beginning of the period in 1914, Americans owed the outside world a net balance of three billions. We were then what is called a "debtor nation," and had been since the Republic was founded. By the end of the period, in 1933, we had switched to the position of a "creditor nation." The world owed us twenty-four billions, minus three billions, or twenty-one billions net. The table shows exactly how the shift took place. The principal reason for the shift was sending more goods abroad than were sent back.

Well, this looks pretty fine. It is better to be a creditor than a debtor any day—at least it used to be. Twenty-one billions to the good. But wait just a minute. About twenty billions will probably never be paid. The ten billions of war debt is virtually a dead loss. Only Finland is keeping up her payments. It is estimated that another ten billions of private debt abroad is uncollectable—loans by American banks, corporations, citizens, to governments and citizens in Germany, Poland, China, Peru, God knows where. If these great debts are not paid—and the prospects never looked blacker than in 1939—then Americans have shipped twenty billion dollars' worth of their soils, crops, manufactured goods abroad with nothing coming back. How did this happen?

A SAD STORY

In the summer of 1914 I was tramping the streets of Rochester looking for any kind of a job. I did not find one. More than 10,000 men were tramping Rochester with me. All over the country, a major depression was forming.

Since the closing of the frontier in 1900, depressions and unemployment were gradually becoming more serious. There was no longer the safety valve of free land in the West. President Wilson might have been forced to do in 1915 some of the things Mr. Hoover and Mr. Roosevelt were forced to do after 1929–inaugurate federal relief, set up a Reconstruction Finance Corporation, enact social security legislation. We might, as a people, really have had to tackle the problem of unemployment *then.* That would have put us two decades farther along in the inevitable adjustments to the power age.

But the war saved us the necessity. It built a temporary prosperity based on the export of food and munitions to the fighting nations. We sold precious little to Germany after the first few months, thanks to the Allies' blockade of the North Sea. Exports to Europe rose from 1.5 billions in 1914 to 3.75 billions in 1916, turning the depression into a war boom.

Most of the goods were sold to the Allied governments. First they paid in gold. Then they paid in American securities. Where did they get the securities? They seized them from their citizens, giving internal government bonds in exchange.

When the gold and securities ran out, they gave I O U's. J. P. Morgan and Company arranged the matter, as fiscal agents for the British and French governments. The governments paid for American wheat and gunpowder with paper promises. American banks discounted the I O U's, giving cash to exporters. President

Wilson had proclaimed early in the war that no "loans" were to be made to belligerents, but he raised no objection to "credits." The I O U's were carefully called "credits" by all concerned.

By January 1, 1917, the "credits" for France and England had climbed to two billion dollars. American bankers began to get cold feet. They would take no more I O U's. Here was a pretty pickle! American factories were all tooled up for war orders, employing millions of workers. American farmers were all tooled up for war shipments of wheat, cotton, livestock. Our whole economy by 1917 was geared to an abnormal war production. If the credits were pulled out, the structure would collapse in panic, bankruptcies and widespread unemployment.

Again, as in 1914, we were saved. Said Walter Hines Page, our Ambassador to England, in March, 1917: "Perhaps our going to war is the only way in which our pre-eminent trade position can be maintained and a panic averted." We declared war on Germany in April. The United States government took over the two billions of "credits" from the banks, and by 1920 had issued eight billions more, making altogether ten billions of war debts due to the Treasury. Accumulated interest has now brought the total to 12.5 billions in 1939. Be sure you see exactly what happened. It is important as a guide to future war "credits," and as an example of the mechanics of foreign trade.

1. American manufacturers and farmers sold food and

munitions to the Allied governments. The governments paid in gold, then in American securities owned abroad.

2. Then American banks took I O U's from the Allied governments, and gave cash to manufacturers and farmers, thus bailing out the manufacturers and farmers.

3. Then the United States government declared war, gave its own bonds to the banks, and took over the I O U's of the Allies, thus bailing out the banks.

4. Then the government took eight billions more of I O U's direct from foreign governments. It sold "Liberty" bonds to you and me. With our cash it paid American manufacturers and farmers eight billions, thus bailing out the Allies.

5. Then the Allied governments found they could not pay their I O U's—and for pretty good reasons, as we shall see—leaving Uncle Sam (meaning you and me) holding the bag. In effect we taxpayers bought ten billions of our countrymen's goods, and presented them to England, France and Italy. We also paid, of course, some thirty billions more for our own war expenditures.

Still, you say, we averted a panic, farmers got good prices for their wheat, manufacturers made money on rifles and chemicals, workers were employed at high wages. True. Well, what is the matter with that? *The matter is that we lost all these goods overseas.* A collateral trouble was that farmers plowed up the Great Plains for more wheat lands, and in due time we reaped the scourge of the dust storm.

If Americans are going to finance Americans to be

prosperous, wouldn't it be a good idea to let Americans consume the output? Those ten billions could have given every family in the country a comfortable house. What happened, as Jerome Frank has pointed out, was a kind of gigantic "public works" program, in which Europe got all the public works. We didn't even get leaves raked—let alone saving the world for democracy.

And that was not the end. After 1920, European soldiers—those that were left—went back to their own wheat fields. American exports declined dizzily, and our agricultural prosperity vanished. Few signs of it have been seen since.

American bankers, however, discovered another splendid "public works" program. We were now a creditor nation. Vice-presidents in big New York banks became owlish experts overnight in Bolivian finance and Polish mining prospects. They were magnificent in their assurance of our manifest destiny. I used to sit enchanted in their offices. Fortunately I was paying for a house at the time, a house in Westchester County, not in Bessarabia.

Investors were urged by all the devices of high pressure selling to make loans to foreign governments, to their subdivisions, and to foreign corporations. As we saw in Mr. Peek's table, another fourteen billions of "credit" was extended. As in the case of war munitions, the money stayed in this country, paying American exporters for goods shipped abroad. This greatly stimulated export trade through the 1920's. The goods we shipped, however, were not always helpful to the home situation, when the books were balanced. Some were used to equip foreign textile mills and shoe factories, destined to compete with our own. Some were used to build American branch plants in foreign countries, another serious source of competition. Some were used for armaments. Some were used for graft. All put a further drain upon our soil and our mineral resources.

This business boomed for six years. Bankers beamed. On each loan they were careful to collect their commissions. Yet the whole procedure was in a financial class with the uproar in Florida swamp lots, which were booming at the same time. The Florida bubble burst in 1926. Foreign lending slowed down in 1928, practically stopped in 1929. Peruvian and Yugo-Slavian "credits" were exhausted. Manufacturers found themselves with factories greatly extended for export business which American investors had been paying for, and now investors were suddenly gun-shy. Foreigners got no more loans. Manufacturers got no more orders. This time the United States government failed to bail them out. They had to close their plants and fire their help. The ranks of the unemployed were swollen from other causes, too —the stock market crash, over-expansion in the plant for domestic business, the collapse of the real estate boom. The great depression was on!

Some ten billions of foreign loans went into the hands of the sheriff after 1929, and another mammoth "public works" program was consummated. Thus a sum not far from twenty billions has vanished since 1914—ten billions in war debts, ten billions in private debts.

Nor is this the end. Since 1933, we have been selling goods for gold. The United States Treasury gives dollars to exporters, takes the gold and buries most of it in a hole in Kentucky. There are about sixteen billions of gold in this country now. But after 1931, nation after nation began to discard the gold standard. Nearly every country in the world is now off gold.[1] Suppose they agree some day to say "to hell with it"? Suppose they refuse to accept gold in foreign trade at all? Jerome Frank thinks this day is coming. If it does, it would leave Uncle Sam, i.e., us taxpayers, holding the bag again, with a mountain of gold worth only what it will fetch for dental work and wedding rings. This would be the equivalent of "public works" program number three in thirty years of foreign trading. It would bring the total handout of free goods to foreigners up to twenty-five or thirty billion dollars' worth.

Please observe that I am not criticizing any group. The Allied governments hoped to remit; American bankers hoped the foreign loans would pay out after the war. There was plenty of stupidity, but little deliberate swindling. Furthermore, Mr. Peek's table had

[1] Meaning that governments refuse to give citizens gold for paper money if they demand it, and often forbid citizens even to keep gold currency.

not been prepared at that time for the enlightenment of international traders.

As a matter of fact, American government policies after the war made it impossible for foreigners to pay off most of their debts. They had to pay in goods; that is the cardinal rule. But this meant increasing American imports, especially manufactured goods, for that is what the people of Europe specialize in producing. American manufacturers set their faces like flint against any such program. They and their employees brought terrific pressure to bear on Congress. Three times the tariff was raised, in 1921, 1922, and to an all-time high in 1930. Not many imports could scale these mighty walls. So what could our European debtors pay with? They did not have enough gold, and we didn't want gold anyway.

A "creditor" nation must arrange for a great inflow of imports if its credits are to be worth anything. England, long a creditor nation, did this by growing less food at home, and importing butter from Denmark, wheat from America, beef from Argentina. We refused to play the creditor game according to the rules. So long as we grow and manufacture most of our supplies at home, it is doubtful whether imports can ever amount to much. By the same token, we shall always lose most of the loans we may make abroad. An excess of exports over imports is known as a "favorable balance of trade." How favorable to the United States are more bad debts or more tons of gold to bury?

So what did Americans get from their excursion into

foreign trade and finance from 1914 to 1933? They got some artificial stimulation which postponed the day of a real reckoning with unemployment and other internal problems. They got a war with 350,000 American dead and wounded, and a cost of some thirty billions to date. They got twenty million grand of bad debts, and presently the finest depression ever known. They lost mountains of good raw materials. They got both agriculture and industry over-extended and thrown out of balance. They got the dust bowl. I hope they got a lesson.

IX. IS FOREIGN TRADE WORTH A WAR?

LET us return to Mr. Peek's table for a moment. In the twenty years from 1914 through 1933, our exports totaled ninety billions. A tidy sum. But in the one year, 1929, the national income of the United States was estimated to be close to ninety billions. The total national income for the twenty years comes to the astronomical figure of 1.2 trillions of dollars. Exports, accordingly, work out to 7.5 per cent of national income, for the whole period. This is a very low ratio as nations go, and confirms the well-known fact that *better than ninety per cent of the American market is inside the country*. Here are some assorted ratios:

Year	*National income* (*In billions*)	*Exports* (*In billions*)	*Per cent*
1913	35.7	2.5	7
1917 (war business) .	51.3	6.2	12
1925	81.9	4.9	6
1930	72.1	3.8	5
1932 (depression low)	40.0	1.6	4
1935	55.2	2.3	4
1936	63.5	2.5	4
1937	69.8	3.3	5

The export ratio jumped, of course, during the war. Since then the trend has been downward. It is now running 4 to 5 per cent of the national income. In England the ratio of exports to national income in recent years has been in the vicinity of 20 per cent; in France, 25 per cent. These continental fragments must have a great volume of foreign trade to keep their people alive. In Russia, the other continental unit, the ratio, like ours, is relatively very low. As Russia equips her new industries, develops cotton fields in Turkestan, it will go lower still.

Another significant feature of our foreign trade is the large proportion of it done with our neighbors in the Western Hemisphere. Trade with Europe, which used to be 60 or 70 per cent of all, is declining. The approximate proportion of export business in recent years has been:

	Per cent
To Canada	16
Latin America	16
Europe	40
Asia and the Pacific	20
All other countries	8
Total	100

Exports are an advantage for some people. At least a million and a half jobs are dependent upon them in this country today. But observe that exports must be offset by an equivalent value of imports, if the rôle of Santa Claus is to be avoided. Certain imports are advantageous for all of us, as we have seen. Failing substitutes, we must have rubber, tin, coffee, and so on, from the outside world. About half of our imports are in the form of raw materials, most of them really needed. The other half are in the form of manufactured goods, many items duplicating the output of home factories.

Not long ago I talked to a man who had just come from Brockton, Massachusetts. Brockton specializes in making boots and shoes. My friend said that as he looked into a store window where shoes imported from Czechoslovakia were on sale, he noticed a line of unemployed men on the street. Now the price or the quality of these Czech shoes may or may not have been attractive, but the fact remains that they were in active competition with shoes made in Brockton. Manufacturers and their workers resented them bitterly.

This is not the place to go into the century-old argument between protection and free trade. That argument took one form when employment was general; it takes quite a different form when unemployment is general. In the latter case, it may be better to keep home workers employed—even if the cost per pair of shoes is higher—than on relief. If we reduce exports we lose some jobs, but the offsetting decline in imports may create some jobs. It is a complicated matter to balance the jobs lost or gained, but it is manifest that export trade is not sheer velvet. When exporters boost their shipments, then importers *must* do likewise—not in twenty-four hours, but sooner or later. Either that, or somebody is going to lose a fortune in foreign loans. The more joy for the exporters, the more gloom, perhaps, for the workers of Brockton. We must also remember that a flood of imports, competing with home products, sometimes drives down wages and living standards. Every reciprocal trade treaty that Mr. Hull signs brings a plaintive howl from some American business men. In New England they were burned up by the recent treaty with old England.

Why must foreign trade be conducted by balancing goods; why can't one party pay in money? That's an easy one. Here is a Japanese textile manufacturer. He wants to buy some cotton from an American exporter. He has plenty of yen, but the exporter can buy nothing with yen in the United States. He wants dollars for his cotton. So the manufacturer goes to his bank in Tokio to swap his yen for dollars. But if the bank has no dollars available, there will be no swap, and no sale. The bank gets dollars primarily by doing business, let us say, with an American importer who wants Japanese silk, and has dollars to pay for it. So the bank swaps these "silk" dollars for the proffered yen, and the Japanese manufacturer buys his cotton with them. Despite all the learned jargon of the international market, *the cotton, in effect, is swapped for the silk.* If the silk does not cross the ocean in one direction, the cotton cannot cross it in the other. Expand this simple principle to include hundreds of commodities, mix in tourists' expenditures and freight charges as tradeable items, add gold as a tradeable item (how long, O Lord?), and you have mastered the broad outlines of foreign exchange. Grasp it, and do not let the experts confound your understanding with uncouth and terrible terms. Confound them instead with Mr. Peek's table.

The United States was a "backward nation" in world markets until after the Civil War. We traded raw materials for manufactured goods—for instance, raw tobacco for cutlery. In 1821, 55 per cent of our imports were manufactured, while only 5 per cent of our exports were the products of our factories. As the years went on, this ratio began to change. By 1910, half of our exports were manufactured goods, many of them competing with manufactures from other industrial nations on the markets of the world.

For a long time England was the chief manufacturing nation, the world's workshop. She gave up growing food, and specialized in workshops. It made her business men rich. But one by one other nations built workshops and began to challenge her lead—France, Belgium, Germany, the United States. Competition in manufactured articles became more and more brisk.

Now observe a profoundly important change in the type of manufactured goods exported. At first such goods were primarily for consumers—cotton cloth, knives, rifles, hardware and the like. But around the turn of the century, business men saw opportunities to make money by exporting *capital goods*, such as textile machinery, steam engines, generators, factory equipment of all kinds. They did not see the inevitable boomerang. It began to hit them or their countrymen soon. The so-called backward nations bought the machinery and set up textile mills, steel plants, boot and shoe factories, paper mills, of their own. Their home labor was often cheap; they undercut exports from the older industrial countries in the home market, and presently they marched out and invaded the world market. Japan, Poland, Brazil, Australia, even India and China, joined the brigade.

First American exporters sold cigarettes to China. Then they sold cigarette-making machinery. Then the Chinese rolled their own. Then they invaded outside markets with cheap, machine-made Chinese cigarettes. Here is the whole story in a nutshell. It happened to scores of articles.

From 1914 to 1928, Japan increased its cotton manufacturing 530 per cent, its wool manufacturing 730 per cent; its paper making 500 per cent; its steel production 570 per cent. From 1911 to 1928, New Zealand enormously increased its output of clothing, hosiery, agricultural machinery and furniture. Between 1916 and 1928, employment doubled in South African factories. In 1903, Argentina established her first shoe factory with equipment from the United States. By 1926, there were 450 modern shoe factories in operation. In 1913, Argentinians imported 1.5 million pairs of shoes; now they import only models. India has more than eight million cotton spindles, China nearly four million—unless the Japanese have bombed them into matchwood.

Advocates of large exports make light of this competition. They say that foreign factories are so small.

and their workers so inefficient, and their inventors so backward, that we can probably outsell them. Will Argentinians throw away their new shoes so that they can have the pleasure of buying from Brockton and Haverhill?

During the 1920's, various United States corporations made competition even more severe by establishing branch plants in foreign countries. These plants naturally sought business. They tried to hold their territory against American competitors as well as against others. "The plain fact is," says Samuel Crowther, "that American manufacturers have already, by expatriating their factories, taken possession of all the sizeable new European markets in sight." The motive of the expatriation was to tunnel under foreign tariff walls. Greetings by foreign manufacturers were not hearty as the American companies emerged from their tunnels. What would the Messrs. Ford, Sloan and Chrysler say if Hitler built a huge branch plant over here to manufacture his new Volkswagen, which will sell for $300 and give forty miles to the gallon? A survey made shortly before war broke out showed at least 1,500 American branch plants operating in foreign countries, employing 250,000 citizens of those countries.

AUTARCHY

Competition was acute before the war. It became savage after 1920. Every trading nation tried to shut off imports by high tariff walls—except, of course, essential raw materials—and to force its own exports on customers by a bewildering variety of high pressure methods. In 1932, thirty-five nations raised their tariffs. Germany issued a special kind of money—blocked marks for foreign trade.[1] Russia tightened her government monopoly of exports and imports. Canada put an embargo on pulpwood; Japan put one on crude camphor to encourage home refineries. Portugal lowered export taxes on goods which traveled in Portuguese ships. England put prohibitive export duties on tin mined in its colonies, in order to build up a monopoly of smelting; and also, for a time, limited the export of rubber from the East Indies—running the price up from fifteen cents to a dollar a pound.

The British, French, Japanese, Italian and Portuguese Empires each arranged a schedule of "imperial preferences," whereby their own and colonial business men were favored over other traders. The United States made a similar arrangement favoring its insular possessions. Exports were subsidized, licensed, subjected to quotas. Bilateral swaps were common, as when Germany would swap manufactured goods for Rumanian oil or wheat. The woods were full of international cartels, jiggling the prices of copper, sugar, manganese and what not. Sometimes the cartels were private, sometimes governmental, sometimes mixed.

To make free trade more painful still, governments tried to encourage self-sufficiency in foodstuffs, thus

[1] Explained in Chapter XII.

cutting down imports of raw materials, and hurting the business of wheat farmers, cotton growers, beef producers, elsewhere. Mussolini staged the great "battle of wheat." By teaching Italian farmers some of Dr. Willcox's intensive agriculture, he rendered the country more nearly self-sufficient in respect to macaroni, spaghetti and bread. The vast Russian markets folded up as Stalin imported tractors and combines, and organized giant farms. France and Germany hold wheat at $1.50 a bushel inside the country, though it can be bought for 75 cents on the world market. Why? To encourage their own peasants to raise more. Artificial fibers, like rayon, cut into the old markets for cotton, wool and silk, while Brazil builds up a great new cotton-growing industry.

In 1926 we exported more than two hundred million bushels of wheat, a quarter of our whole crop. In 1933 we exported forty million bushels, a twentieth of the crop. When an American business man tried to unload some wheat on Brazil the other day, the Argentine government made a vigorous protest. Why ship wheat thousands of miles when Argentina had a big surplus right next door?

We used to supply sixty per cent of the world's cotton. Now we supply about forty per cent. England, Japan, India have enormously reduced their purchases. Our exports of leaf tobacco, cotton, meat, salmon, wheat, phosphates, petroleum, copper, were all less in 1936 than in 1914—twenty-two years earlier. Secretary

Hull's reciprocal trade treaties may have created some good will but they have had little effect on tonnage movement.

Up to 1914, world trade was increasing. Tariffs were common, but export restrictions were rare; the gold standard was all but universal, and trade was relatively free. Competition was keen, especially in manufactured goods. The old industrial nations were exporting capital goods at an increasing rate. Business men did the trading. During the war, the belligerent governments monopolized foreign trade in order to insure supplies of food and munitions. After the war, government controls were slightly relaxed, but the old free market did not return. What is called economic nationalism, "autarchy," became the order of the day. Each nation tried to increase its self-sufficiency, to restrict its imports, to stimulate its exports.

They were preparing for a day when supplies would be desperately needed, with little to spare in exchange. That day has now come for the belligerents. By blockade, embargo and direct attack, they strive to cut off each other's shipping. Every home-grown crop, every *ersatz* factory, saves precious tonnage. Neutral traders stand to profit—as long as they keep neutral and afloat. Small European neutrals that are not self-sufficient find themselves on a spot today.

Another reason for autarchy is machine technology, the equipment of once backward nations with machines of their own, and many new inventions in synthetic products, have all made for increased self-sufficiency and more competition in manufactured goods. Autarchy would have been inevitable, war or no war. It will continue, as we saw in Chapter VII, unless scientists and inventors are suppressed. Thus there are good reasons, both in current conditions and in the long term trend, why world trade should halt and export markets grow narrower. It is hard to see how the trend can be reversed. Secretary Hull is doing his best, but it is probably too late.

If a nation *must* trade, as the nations of Europe must, for large stocks of raw materials, there is little to do but accept the situation and go in for blocked marks, imperial preferences and bilateral swaps. But if a continental family of nations, like the United States, does not need a great volume of external trade to supply its citizens, it is downright foolish to imitate less fortunate neighbors.

OUR STAKE ABROAD

The stake of American citizens abroad is not great. The gross figure, including war debts, is under thirty billions—a third of the national income in one good year. But the war debts must be written off in large part, and also some ten billions of private debt. That leaves a net active and collectable investment of less than ten billion. The best of this investment, furthermore, is in Canada, the Caribbean countries and South America.

The total American investment in China today is about 132 millions, with another forty millions in missionary property. Harry Hopkins often spent as much as this in one month, when he put his mind on it. England's investment in China is six times as great as ours. The total of our export trade is now about one twentieth of our national income; of this only less than two per cent goes to China—a tiny proportion of the national income. If we go to war for the Open Door in China, it will be for sentimental reasons, not commercial. The costs of a few days of war would offset all the profits that business men can make out of China in the next generation.

In 1930, before the bad debts were written off, the stake abroad, other than government war loans, was estimated by Louis Hacker as follows:

	In billions, 1930			
	Direct investment, branch plants, etc.	*Stocks, bonds, notes, etc.*	*Total*	*Per cent*
Canada	2.1	1.9	4.0	25
Mexico, Central America and Caribbean	2.0	.6	2.6	16
South America	1.6	1.4	3.0	19
Total New World	5.7	3.9	9.6	60
Europe	1.5	3.4	4.9	30
Far East and Asia	.6	.9	1.5	9
Africa	.1	..	.1	1
Total	7.9	8.2	16.1	100

Remember that much of this is now in the sheriff's hands.

Note how our stake in the New World was sixty per cent of our total of foreign investments, and twenty-five per cent was in Canada alone. The stake in the Old World was 6.5 billions, of which probably only a small fraction is collectable.

Remember, too, that Japan is likely to lose her silk trade with us, when Mr. du Pont's factories begin to produce the new synthetic fiber. This means that we must lose an offsetting amount of exports to Japan. If silk does not come over, then cotton cannot go back.

All the figures point to a stalemate in export trade—too many machines; too much competition; too much economic nationalism; too many government controls. This makes a critical situation for the British Empire, which grew great on the free market of the nineteenth century—the market that Mr. Hull looks back to so fondly. At the same time, it makes Hitler's drive for colonies and world markets seem pretty silly. A drive for self-sufficiency is understandable, but for a commercial empire it is about thirty years too late. The British commercial empire is rapidly weakening, not because English business men have lost their grip, but because the trading system which nourished it is passing from the world picture. Does Hitler want to take over that ancient carryall and die out too?

Grabbing territory, enslaving natives, was all very well for Alexander, Attila, Genghis Khan—even for Cecil Rhodes. We have largely progressed beyond that sort of thing today. It is difficult to grow rich by owning colonies which cost more, in administrative and naval expenses, than trading rights can ever return. Some business men can make money out of the colonies, but home taxpayers lose more than the business men gain. It is difficult or impossible to "enslave" a territory equipped with a modern industrial plant. Slaves do not do the work; machines do it. Mussolini made a spirited march into Ethiopia in the best Kitchener and Kipling tradition. He won the war and lost his shirt. Italian taxpayers will know what I mean. Japan's march into China may have a similar result. Both Ethiopia and China are classed as backward countries. A march into an industrial area, smashing the delicate arteries of power, transport and supply which tie the community together, can have only the most calamitous results for victor as well as vanquished. Notions of territorial expansion, booty, gold, enslaving populations, belong with the rape of the Sabine women, plausible enough in its own age and context but fantastic in high energy societies. Some modern dictators seem to think in these antiquated and grandiose terms. They may march out on the strength of them to burn and ravage. Millions will die, but no elephants will parade, bringing back Nubians, spices, jewels and lovely Gothic women. France and England won the war in 1918. Look at their people and their economic situation today.

"After the collapse of the economic structure in 1929," says Dr. Beard, "a conception of national interest in foreign commerce appeared—a concept that a high standard of national well-being is possible with a minimum reliance on foreign trade; and is desirable besides." If citizens of the United States limited trade to those items which were needed to maintain living standards, we should largely cease to be fighting competitors in perilously shrunken export markets. Pressure would be reduced by that much. We should be viewed with respect, even be considered as *benefactors.* We should set an example of what a strong self-contained people could do. If we have surpluses to dump, we had better follow Mr. Wallace's suggestion, and dump them at home. Why subsidize gifts to foreigners, or create angry neighbors by increasing export competition? There are plenty of Americans on relief who could use more wheat, cotton goods, and electrical appliances. If markets must be subsidized, subsidize at home.

Imports must balance exports in the long run. There is a rule for statesmen here, if we dig deep enough:

The dollar value of such imports as are really essential to the national economy, should determine the dollar value of exports.

Let a committee of experts figure out what we must have in the way of rubber, tin, coffee and the rest, plus what may be advisable to import in order to conserve natural resources. Then let the government announce the total, perhaps issuing export licenses for a like amount, allocated among producers of real surpluses. You may call this regimentation if you wish, but it makes a lot of sense. My guess is that this rule is destined to dominate the field of foreign trade all over the world in the years before us.

How much do Americans need today in the way of essential imports? Not far from the actual money total in recent years, as a matter of fact. A billion and a half would probably cover it. A policy of blindly pushing exports much beyond that invites international friction, uncollectable loans, free gifts of "public works."

Naturally American exporters welcome the orders brought them by the ill wind of this war. The financial editors of newspapers gloat over the South American markets to which we are falling heir, over "benefits" to producers of oil, aircraft, motors, chemicals and many other items. A few headaches come with the benefits—questions of shipping, freight rates, war-risk insurance, and the grisly possibility with each shipment that cargo, crew and vessel may go to the bottom.

Some business men of course will profit and unemployment will be reduced. Few business men pause to inquire what new imports will balance the new exports, or how equilibrium can be restored when the war ends, or what will be done with the growing cellarful of gold in Kentucky.

X. A POLICEMAN FOR THE PLANET

THERE is something about the term "internationalism" which stirs emotion in many hearts. It calls up the age-old idea of the brotherhood of man. The great religions cross national and continental boundaries. Socialists sing a famous song, *The International*. It is a high-minded word, but actual international traffic is a mixed affair.

To dump shoddy goods on a neighbor nation is not particularly high-minded—say boots made of paper, or adulterated rum for consumption by natives. The international armament ring leaves something to be desired in terms of brotherhood. If two countries combine to exploit a third, the angels are not necessarily pleased. England and Russia once divided up Persia. Poland is now being partitioned for the fourth time. Free trade in highly competitive manufactured articles often leads to bitterness rather than friendship.

We are likely to disappear in a verbal fog if we try to make a clean-cut distinction between "internationalism" as always beneficent, and "nationalism" as always selfish. To give these terms meaning, we must break them down into real activities in the world outside the tidy patterns in our heads. We must ask: What kind of internationalism? When was it functioning? Where was it functioning? Do you refer to the internationalism of the Roman Empire in 100 A.D.; the internationalism of the Catholic

Church in 1200 A.D.; of Napoleon in 1810; of the Holy Alliance in 1823; of the British Empire; of the world market in the nineteenth century; of the League of Nations; of the Olympic games; of the white slave trade; of the Third International of the communists?

We can recognize two great tendencies in traffic and intercourse between nations today. On the one hand, the peoples of the world are continually being knit more closely together by scientific progress in communication and transportation. Just think how all the world followed Mr. Chamberlain to Munich, on the radio. In what the anthropologists call "culture," nations increasingly resemble one another. Standards in dress, manners, scientific procedure, educational methods, weights and measures, art, music, literature, games, grow more uniform. In mountain villages in Mexico, to which even a horse could hardly climb, let alone a truck, I have seen brown boys in big sombreros playing baseball. No influence in the direction of uniformity is more powerful than American films.

In economic traffic, on the other hand, as noted earlier, the tide now runs in the opposite direction. The march of the inventors is creating more and more possibilities of self-sufficiency. In addition, the governments of the several nations since the war, have, in their fear of new wars, turned from the old free market. International trade approaches a dead level if not a decline.

Let us draw up a list of various kinds of international traffic, in an attempt to clarify the concept:

INTERNATIONAL TRAFFIC: DESIRABLE

Exchange of travelers and tourists. International hospitality.

Air travel, without bombs.

Standard rules for navigation; lighthouses, buoys, charts, S O S wave-bands.

Stabilized currencies.

Standards for weights and measures. The metric system.

Postal unions. Copyright agreements.

Telephone, telegraph and cable communication.

Radio. But playing down the propaganda.

Exchange of films, especially documentary. Television.

An international language. Basic English or even Esperanto.

Exchange of art, music, literature, drama.

Olympic games, Davis cups for tennis, other sports. Rotary Clubs.

Exchange of university students and professors.

International labor standards; the work of the I.L.O. at Geneva.

International public health work. Control of epidemics. Relief in famine and disaster. The Red Cross. The Rockefeller Foundation.

Exchange of scientific information. Scientific congresses. The World Power Conference.

Exchange of patents and new technical processes.

World's Fairs.

Exchange of necessary raw materials.

International arbitration machinery. The World Court.

INTERNATIONAL TRAFFIC: UNDESIRABLE

The exploitation of workers and raw materials in backward nations. Imperialism. Dollar Diplomacy.

Trade in highly competitive manufactured goods.

Loans abroad that will never be paid.

Loans abroad for armaments.

International armament rings.

International slave trade, white slavery, narcotic trade. (England once fought a war to keep the opium traffic open to her business men.)

Spy systems.

Secret treaties and alliances.

Propaganda agencies—especially organizations with guns and colored shirts. It is dangerous enough to have them at home.

Anti-Semitism.

INTERNATIONAL TRAFFIC: DESIRABILITY DEPENDING ON CIRCUMSTANCES

International gold standard. Good in 1900, difficult in 1940.

International banking.

Loans for development of backward countries.

International cartels and monopolies.

Migrations and changes of nationality. Jews must have somewhere to live. The United States needed immigrants until 1910; it needs few today when unemployment is severe.

Diplomatic corps. Sometimes useful and sometimes mischievous.

Trade in raw materials. See both categories above.

World-wide religions and ideologies. Yes and no. The modern roster includes, among others, Catholicism, Mohammedanism, Naziism, Italian fascism, communism, Judaism, political democracy, Social Credit, the Single Tax, the Co-operative Commonwealth, Buchmanism, Christian Science.

These lists are not intended to be complete, but only to suggest how "internationalism" can be classified into some of the actual movements of men, materials and ideas which pass from land to land. It is foolish to call oneself a 100 per cent "internationalist," "isolationist," devotee of "collective security," when traffic among nations takes so many forms. If you go down the list checking those items which you favor, and those which you do not, you will forever cease to consider yourself a chemically pure "internationalist" or "isolationist."

THE RISE AND FALL OF THE LEAGUE OF NATIONS

The idea of a parliament of the world is very ancient. The idea of the "sovereign state" is comparatively recent, as Dr. Beard has demonstrated. Poets, priests, writers, have long urged that the several peoples bury their hatchets and enter one big wigwam.

In 1899, and again in 1907, the Czar invited representatives of the powers to meet at The Hague and plan for peace. (Between these dates he got into an unfortunate mixup with the Mikado.) An arbitration tribunal was set up (long before the World Court) to adjust differences between nations. A few unimportant quarrels were referred to the Tribunal and settled. But the Great Powers are rarely disposed to arbitrate what their leaders think are important quarrels. As Earl Russell said over half a century ago in the Alabama case: "That is a question of honor which we will never arbitrate, for England's honor can never be made a subject of arbitration." (Mr. Chamberlain arbitrated as long as he could.) Bryan, as Secretary of State in 1913, made arbitration treaties with thirty nations, in which the high contracting parties solemnly agreed to wait a year before going to war—thus giving diplomats, generals and citizens a chance to cool off.

The League of Nations has been the chief exhibit in international machinery in our time. President Wilson wanted a strong League, backed by an international police force, and founded on a just peace, in which no belligerent should be called guilty of starting the war. When Mr. Lloyd George and M. Clemenceau finished revising Mr. Wilson's plan, he got a paper League, with no police force, based on a grossly unjust peace treaty, with Germany specifically blamed for starting the war.

All nations were supposed to be represented, but the United States Senate refused to permit President Wilson to join his own League. It was further felt that the morals of Germany and Russia were such that the delegates of the Allied Powers could not sit around a conference table with Huns and Bolsheviks. So the League began its labors with three of the seven Great Powers outside. England and France dominated the executive committee of the Inner Council. Their delegates were naturally interested in maintaining the status quo, in keeping intact their war gains and the war losses of Germany and Austria.

Even with this inauspicious beginning, the League turned in a reasonably good performance for some years. In 1926, Germany was deemed to be sufficiently disinfected, and was allowed to join. Indemnity payments were scaled down. The French army got out of the Rhineland. Russia was washed and admitted. Briand and Stresemann behaved like a pair of real world statesmen. Several little wars were halted by League action; a bitter argument between Finland and Sweden was settled. Some fine work was done in controlling typhus epidemics, and in checking the opium and white slave traffic. The collection of world statistics was altogether admirable. Many of the figures used in these pages come from the League's *Statistical Year Book*. Outside the official League, a series of disarmament conferences delayed the building of battleships, if not of tanks and airplanes. The Nine Power Treaty, guaranteeing the territorial integrity of China, was signed in 1922, and the Kellogg peace pacts in 1928.

Soon after the depression of 1929, however, these hopeful beginnings faltered. The League was a fair weather sailor. Japan took advantage of the depression to invade Manchuria. Mr. Stimson, our Secretary of State, offered to proceed under the Nine Power Treaty, to preserve Manchuria from virtual annexation. The League, in the person of Sir John Simon, refused to co-operate, leaving Mr. Stimson high and dry with a very red face. The United States, a non-member, had taken the initiative in a League task, only to be shown the door. British statesmen did not want to take a strong line in Manchuria. So the Japanese army went ahead and seized it.

In 1935 came the second great test. Mussolini proposed to annex Ethiopia. Ethiopia was a member of the League. So was Italy at the time. This was a little like grandpa eating little Johnnie at the family dinner table. The League had no police force, but it was authorized to use economic "sanctions"–meaning that members must refuse to furnish Italy with supplies. Again the United States government offered to co-operate and employ sanctions too; "only to find," says Hamilton Fish Armstrong, "that Great Britain and France had no intention of making their threats effective." Again we were left high and dry, with red faces.

About this time, the League tried to settle the war in the Gran Chaco between Bolivia and Paraguay. An embargo was imposed on Paraguay. The United States–still not a member–adhered to the embargo. But League members turned it into a farce by open smuggling.

Then came the Civil War in Spain. The League did nothing, and French and English statesmen did worse. Then came the invasion of China by Japan in 1937. The League passed a pious resolution. Then came Hitler's seizure of Austria and the partition of Czechoslovakia, both contrary to the solemn covenants which the League was founded to uphold. By this time nobody even paged Geneva.

Mr. Chamberlain laid a wreath upon the tomb. He said: "The League of Nations, as constituted today, is unable to provide collective security for anybody. . . . We must not try to delude small and weak nations into thinking that they will be protected by the League against aggression . . . when we know that nothing of the kind can be expected."

That leaves the United States, as Hubert Herring has pointed out, the only Galahad remaining to save the world for the righteous. It is a chilly task. This melancholy fragment of history, however, is valuable in the negative sense. It teaches us what a real League *must not do*. M. Clemenceau's League broke down because:

1. It did not include *all* the Great Powers.

2. There was no surrender of sovereignty by the members. At a pinch, any member could refuse to cooperate.

3. There was no world policeman. In Article VIII,

President Wilson wanted the armaments of all members reduced to the lowest point consistent with *domestic* safety; that is, an army only large enough to cope with riots inside the country. The statesmen of the Allies changed "domestic" to "national" safety; that is, an army large enough to lick the world—if you could afford it. It is remarkable what diplomats and generals can do with such a roomy term as national safety.

4. The League was pledged to the status quo as defined by the Treaty of Versailles. The lessons to be learned from history are not many, but certainly one of them is that national frontiers the world over do not remain very long unchanged. A real League must be prepared to make economic as well as political adjustments, insuring the so-called "have-not" peoples an adequate amount of raw materials.

The editor of a newspaper in Oklahoma once told me the story of how law and order came to his town. It was a pioneer cow town, and then oil was struck. This made for rugged individualism, in all senses of the term. Every citizen was a sovereign power unto himself. He maintained his territorial integrity and national honor, with a six-shooter. That is, he maintained it as long as he survived. Peaceful citizens spent their time dodging bullets. The town became a shambles. Orderly business was impossible. At last the citizens revolted. They organized a league. They appointed a sheriff and a committee to assist him. They saw that both were well supplied with munitions. My friend devoted his paper to advocating the league. Night after night he wrote editorials, with a Winchester across the desk. Twice bullets came through the editorial window, and one went through his hat. The sheriff was killed, but another promptly took office. It was a hard fight, but the league won. From then on quarrels were settled by the judge, and if there was any shooting to be done, the sheriff did it.

Analogies are always dangerous, but there may be a moral here somewhere. This sounds all right in Oklahoma, but a bit Utopian in world affairs. Neither Mr. Hitler, Mr. Chamberlain, Mr. Stalin, the Japanese General Staff, nor the Senate of the United States, is going to surrender national sovereignty to a super-state until the world is either much more disorderly or much more orderly than it is now. With world armament outlays at eighteen billions in 1938, no government is turning in its guns to any world sheriff.

The chances for a real League look dismal enough as I write. Speaking as a citizen, I hope my government will not run around signing up with half-leagues and quarter-leagues like Geneva, which may only make international traffic worse. The United States can *initiate* a plan for a real League. Mr. H. S. Raushenbush, in his book *The Final Choice*, draws an admirable first draft. We might before long start a League of the West, for the nations of the New World. But we can afford to wait if the Old World is not ready. Any partnership with Mr. Chamberlain would obviously be a two per cent affair. A League with one or another of the Great Powers would probably leave us paying the bills as heretofore, and our young men dead on foreign soil. I feel strongly about this, for I have a son of military age.

When England, Germany, France, Russia, Japan, Italy, all agree to go in together, and will in fact reduce their armies and navies to the demands of internal riot calls; when the surplus armaments are turned over to an international policeman; when arrangements are made for a fair exchange of essential raw materials—then let us go in and co-operate to the limit. There is some risk, but chances have to be taken in this world.

Most of the smaller nations entered the old League with enthusiasm. Their people would doubtless be glad to form a better one. They cannot protect themselves now against the military might of any of the Great Powers. If this war should last a long time, the exhausted belligerents might possibly be ready to join a stronger league. A splendid one could probably be organized with such nations as Finland, Holland, Denmark, Switzerland, Sweden, Norway, Argentina, Chile, Mexico. Together the smaller countries have more people than the Great Powers, and their governments appear to have more horse sense. Some of them—Holland, Spain, Portugal, Sweden—were once Great Powers, and have given it up as a bad job. It is the Seven Big Brutes, with dictators and statesmen all too frequently burning with a lust for world dominion, that chiefly jam the machinery. We are one of the seven. But since the passing of McKinley and Theodore Roosevelt, we have had no leading statesmen looking for world dominion. We have all the dominion we can take care of here in North America.

Men have survived, progressed and been happy without nationalism, in the past, and they can do it again. They have worked their way out of the institutions of slavery and witchcraft. Some day they will work their way out of international anarchy. All men of good will look forward to the World State. But looking does not mean that it is here. We in America had better not act as if it were here. Let us work and pray for it, but keep our powder dry.

XI. THE PRICE OF PEACE

WHEN the German army marched into Belgium in 1914, President Wilson promptly announced that the United States was to remain neutral. Such had been our policy for one hundred years. If Gallup polls had been available in those days, it is safe to say that 98 per cent of the voters would have been found to agree with the President.

Under the rules of international law, neutral nations had the right to trade with belligerents, and their citizens had the right to travel on the merchant ships of belligerents. We began to ship supplies to the Allies and to Germany. In November, 1914, the British navy closed the North Sea. No more supplies could go to Germany, or even to Norway and Sweden, where they might be transshipped to Germany. American vessels were stopped, searched, and turned back. The Allies prepared the famous "black list" of contraband goods, which included 90 per cent of all commodities shipped in foreign trade. These high-handed decrees were contrary to the doctrine of freedom of the seas. The American government made many protests, but they did no good.

In retaliation for the blockade, the Germans launched the U-boat campaign. Submarines set out from their bases in German ports, dove under the British battleships, to appear off the coast of Ireland and torpedo vessels loaded with supplies for the Allies. This constituted an even more serious affront to the freedom of the seas. A ship is sailing peacefully along, headed for Southampton. Suddenly her people feel a sickening thud deep down inside the hull. They have only a few minutes to take to the boats. Often many are drowned. The cargo goes to the bottom. Millions of tons of shipping were thus sunk.

President Wilson protested to the German government, but received no more satisfaction than from the British government. *This was war,* not polite exercises in international law. American citizens, meanwhile, were traveling freely on Allied merchantmen. Often these vessels carried munitions. The Allies liked to have American passengers, who acted as virtual hostages, making submarine commanders more careful of their torpedoes. Germany, at least in the beginning, was not eager to have the United States added to her enemies. In the case of the *Lusitania,* loaded with ammunition and American citizens, the caution of the Germans was unfortunately relaxed. The great liner went to the bottom, munitions, Americans and all. Some historians believe that the Allies were deliberately careless in warning the *Lusitania's* captain, hoping that the tragedy would shock the American people into war. It worked out that way.

As we saw earlier, the export trade stimulated by the war saved us from a serious business depression. Sales of explosives to Europe in 1914 were ten millions; in 1916 they climbed to 715 millions. Business boomed. Farmers were happy. Unemployed men got jobs. Profits of all American corporations rose from an average of 4.1 billions in 1911-1913, to an average of 6.9 billions in 1914-1916. A great vested interest in war prosperity grew up.

Meanwhile, with the German cables cut, only one brand of propaganda reached the United States. German lies were few and feeble; Allied lies were many and strong. The British quickly grasped the necessity of winning American good will, both to insure supplies, and to draw the United States in as a military ally in due time. Sir Gilbert Parker was appointed as chief wizard. He lined up such skilled literary men as Kipling, Wells, Galsworthy, Bennett, and even, until he could stand it no longer, George Bernard Shaw. Barrie was sent over to lecture. Lord Bryce, the famous author of *The American Commonwealth*, was commandeered. The British Trades Union Congress went to work on the leaders of the American Federation of Labor. Theodore Roosevelt, Senator Lodge, Elihu Root, "Marse" Henry Watterson, were natural pushovers. They, and many other members of the American aristocracy, had always looked to England as the mother country; the home of culture and of the code of the gentleman. The *New York Times*, with its powerful editorial page, abandoned neutrality at an early date.

"Democracy" was played up heavily; the awkward fact that Czarist Russia was fighting with the Allies was played down. Colonel House and Secretary Lansing, as Walter Millis has shown in his *Road to War*, were convinced that we ought to join England and France, and they kept their point of view constantly before President Wilson. Horrible stories of German atrocities came out of the propaganda mill. Most of them were subsequently proved to be without foundation. It was said that the Kaiser had a base in Mexico, and was planning to seize Texas and set up a black republic with the help of Negroes and Mexicans. Bernhardi, Treitschke —German writers little read at home—were discovered by the propaganda staff, and their brutal philosophies were spread all over America as typical samples of German thought.

The propaganda had to be astute, for the Allies were desperately afraid that the United States government would demand a peace without victory. In 1916, Germany was said to be ready for such a settlement. The Allies were afraid of committing themselves to a statement of war aims. They had secret treaties with one another, giving the Czar Constantinople, and distributing fragments of the Austro-Hungarian Empire to the victors. The treaties were diametrically opposed to President Wilson's war aims. So the problem was to get us in without disclosing what they were really after.

We have to take off our hats to them. They did it. The sinking of the *Lusitania* turned many American neutrals and pacifists toward war. The official cause of our entry was interference with American shipping, by submarines. A Gallup poll on April 1, 1917, would probably still have shown a majority of American citizens against war. It was too late. The voters had no voice. With the best of intentions, we had blundered in so deep that we couldn't get out. And President Wilson, in his study at the White House that fateful night, knew with a terrible clarity that democracy and freedom would not be saved.

There were three relentless forces which thrust us into war: The pressure of *financial* involvement in trade and loans; the pressure of *legal* involvement in the hopeless attempt to maintain the rights of neutral ships and citizens, and the freedom of the seas; the *emotional* pressure generated by the propaganda of the Allies, with little to offset it from the other camp.

Just by way of reference, here are some of the slogans that capsized us in 1917 and strengthened our morale after we got in. It will be interesting to compare them with the crop generated in the world war of 1939.

A scrap of paper
Poor little Belgium
Poor little Serbia
The rights of small nations
Freedom of the seas
Open covenants, openly arrived at
The war to end war
A war against Militarism
A war against Autocracy
A war to make the world safe for Democracy
The Allies are fighting our war
Where would we be without the British navy?
Self-determination
Make Germany pay
Hang the Kaiser
Berlin or bust

A BALANCE SHEET

No one knows how long the new world war will last, or how many nations will be involved. In respect to freedom of the seas, it began where the old war left off. In the first two weeks, thirty ships were sunk by German torpedoes, or British shells, or by striking mines. Both sides have instituted savage blockades designed to starve each other out. Heaven help neutral shipping, and the rules of international law, caught between this terrible cross-fire.

Once again voices are raised about the solemn duty of America to join the Allied cause. Suppose we try to cast a balance sheet of what it will cost us if we go to war.

If We Go In

The federal debt, now standing at some forty billions, will jump twenty, thirty, perhaps fifty billions in two or three years. Last time it jumped twenty-six billions in about two years. If the war is prolonged it may pass one hundred billions. War debts due by our Allies will reach astronomical figures, and of course can never be paid.

These untold billions will be spent, not for implements of life but for implements of death. But by virtue of the spending, a huge war boom will be generated. Between the call for conscripts and the call for workers in munitions factories, unemployment will practically disappear. Prices will rise, the cost of living will go up, the stock market will soar. Capital outlays for such public improvements as housing, conservation, health centers, will all but cease. Capital will flow into armament factories, and possibly into fleets of tractors to rip open the sod of the Great Plains again and revive the dust storms. Precious deposits of oil, iron, lead, zinc, copper, will be depleted at an appalling rate.

The War Department is all ready for the next war with its "M Day" program. The program calls for immediate conscription of all men between 21 and 31. The rest of us will be told what and how much to eat, what to wear, at what temperature to heat our houses. The railroads will be commandeered, wages and prices fixed by fiat, foreign trade made a government monopoly. A tax of 95 per cent will be imposed upon all profits above the average of the last three years. The government will license business concerns, stimulating some, closing down others. If a business man objects to having his company turned inside out, it will be taken over by a government corporation. Not a dollar can be legally invested without permission. The banks will be socialized, in fact if not in name; also, probably, the insurance companies. Interest rates will be fixed by decree. Farmers will be told what to grow. To strike will be a criminal offense. Gasoline purchases will be restricted by rationing cards. You will be allotted so much electric power, and all lights out at ten o'clock.

These powers will be exercised by an organization to be called the Advisory Defense Council. It will supersede the regular Cabinet, and be answerable only to the

Commander-in-Chief of the Army and Navy—namely, the President. Except for the insertion of dates, titles and salaries, legislation for starting the economic war machine in motion has been drafted. When war comes, Congress will pass the act. That will be the last heard from Congress, or from the Supreme Court.

A thorough-going state socialist could ask nothing better than M Day to further his cause. If you think the case overstated, I suggest that you study what has already happened in France and England. If we go to war in a style to befit the world's most powerful nation, we can say good-by to political democracy, the Bill of Rights and private enterprise for a long, long time.

Censorship will be adamant, radio will become a state monopoly, the press will be muzzled, free speech abolished. Dictatorial rule may continue long after the war ends. Private business as we know it will shrink to a wizened stump. Mr. Roosevelt, whether he likes it or not, may be drafted for life. We have at present no other leaders of his stature. The war, and the terrifying depression which must follow the war, will imperatively demand leadership.

If we fight Germany, we shall be forced to fight her allies. At the present writing she claims Russia as an ally, while Russia is concluding an understanding with Japan. International treaties are tender blossoms, to be sure, but we might end up with not only Germany on our hands, but Russia, Japan, Italy, Turkey, Hungary, and all manner of folks with whom we have no quarrel. Being

Americans, once we got into it we should want to see it through—if we had to take on half the world. God knows on how many foreign shores our boys would be buried, and how many hundreds of thousands of them.

If we help France and England to win a relatively short war, we shall certainly be called upon to guarantee the peace which terminates it. As Colonel Lindbergh suggested, that puts us bag and baggage into European power politics, perhaps so deep that we can never get out. We shall enter the war saying, "Never again a Versailles treaty," but after two or three years of hatred, atrocities, reprisals, sinkings and bombings of women and children, we shall feel differently. Versailles might be a love pat compared to the ferocious provisions of the Treaty of Liverpool. When in due course new Hitlers arise, we shall have to do it all over again.

If We Stay Out

If we avoid war, and enact the neutrality program shortly to be presented—or something like it—the picture will be very different. We shall have a moderate boom in business, a small increase in federal debt, no more war debts to embitter our foreign relations, a continuation of investment in public improvements rather than in engines of destruction. Government controls will probably expand a little, but our economy will not be twisted into state socialism overnight. We shall continue along the middle road of gradual economic change. Unemployment will not decline so rapidly as if we went to war, but we shall have much slighter adjustments to make after the fighting ends. We shall build up no consuming hatreds, we shall make no commitments to guarantee the reeling boundary lines of Europe. We may be in a position to act as mediator when an exhausted Europe can fight no longer. We shall not risk taking on half the world in mortal combat. Political democracy will be maintained and regular elections held. Fellow citizens will not be tortured because they were born with German names. We shall miss a sense of national unity, and the savage thrill of winning victories. We shall also miss the grim experience of defeats, and of mounting casualty lists.

HOW TO BE NEUTRAL

Most Americans want to be neutral. They have sensed the purport of this balance sheet, even if they have not written it out in black and white. On September 17, 1939, a Gallup poll showed 84 per cent of the country against sending armies to fight abroad.

"Neutrality" is a word employed to cover various sorts of behavior. When people discuss it without careful definition, they become badly confused. There are at least three distinct concepts for the term—let us call them Neutrality A, Neutrality B, Neutrality C.

Neutrality A we may define as rigorously *impartial* behavior. Try not to give the slightest advantage to either belligerent. Try to keep words and even thoughts impartial. Neutrality A is a counsel of perfection. Few individuals can help favoring one side or the other in a baseball game, a boxing match, or a war. No government can help assisting one side or the other quite unintentionally.

Neutrality B we may define as behavior which avoids supplying belligerents with lethal weapons. This is a moral concept; it implies that we don't want to be classed as "merchants of death." It is obvious that this concept, to be consistent, ought to be applied in peace time as well as in war time. A bomb shipped before September first is just as deadly as one shipped after hostilities began.

Neutrality C we may define as behavior guided by the *sole aim of keeping the United States out of this war.* If we focus on this concept, the air is cleared. We give up trying to see how impartial we can be, or how moral we can be.

After investigating the munitions industry for a year or more, Congress passed a Neutrality Act. The stench of the arms traffic was revolting to most citizens. The Act put an embargo on shipments of arms to belligerents. This clause makes us feel cleaner, but does it help to keep us out of war? I cannot see that it does, or even that this was the chief intention of its framers. Congress was concerned with Neutrality B, not with Neutrality C. If the Allies cannot buy arms from us, they may redouble their propaganda efforts to get us to fight on their side. But if the embargo is lifted, Germany may redouble her efforts to sink all shipments of munitions to the Allies, thus involving American lives and property. There is a threat of war either way.

If we stick to Neutrality C we turn in a different direction altogether. Instead of worrying about who gets arms or doesn't get them, we try to prevent American lives and property from standing in the path of stray projectiles. We also try to avoid a huge vested interest in exports. These are the two major dangers of involvement, as the last war showed: destruction of our shipping by submarines, the pressure of a profit-mad export traffic.

The strictly logical course would be to call home all citizens and cut off all exports, except to nations completely outside the zone of combat. If none of our property and none of our citizens could get in a position where they might be seized, sunk or blown up, the danger of going to war to protect our rights would be remote. Such a course, though theoretically possible, would cause a great deal of internal trouble—unemployment, business losses, shortages in imported raw materials. It is probably too heroic for a practical policy.

Almost the same end can be achieved by restoring the cash and carry provision of the law and making it mandatory. This means that our goods are paid for at American ports; title passes to the foreign buyer, and he takes them away in his own ship. If the ship is sunk, we have no claims to make against anybody, for neither the goods, the ship, nor the crew is American. The cash and carry proviso can be applied with or without the embargo on arms. Personally, I should like to see the munitions trade halted, but if you asked me to define what items constitute munitions, I could not do it. Cotton can be made into bandages or into explosives. Scrap steel can be made into plows or into shrapnel.

If it is argued that cash and carry is unneutral because only the Allies have cash and can do the carrying, we reply that we are not defining neutrality as impartiality—any more than Sweden did in 1914. Cash and carry may or may not operate as an impartial device, but that isn't the point. Will it tend to involve the United States in war? It will not—which *is* the point.

What happens when the cash runs out? Here is another danger zone. After the Allies have spent all their loose change in a hurry, Congress will be stormed by business men and farmers to permit loans. The Neutrality Law forbids loans to any belligerent. Pressure to repeal this may be terrific. So it would be an excellent idea to rule that shipments of any given commodity to belligerents shall not be more than a fourth higher than average annual shipments for the last three years. This would forestall a wild boom in war exports and the building up of vested interests, which would bring pressure to bear for loans when the cash expired. It would also prevent expanding our economy for an export trade sure to collapse with a sickening thud when the shooting stops.

Here are the elements of what I consider a real neutrality program. It is, I think, good for this war or any war.

1. Forbid all long-term credit to belligerents.

2. Place all exports to belligerents on a cash and carry basis.

3. Restrict exports to belligerents to a quota based on average sales for the last three years, plus twenty-five per cent, or some such reasonable figure. This applies to all exports, munitions or otherwise. Whether munitions should be embargoed is primarily a moral question, and outside the scope of this program.

4. Accumulate stock piles of essential raw materials not available in the United States, especially tin and rubber.

5. Forbid American ships to enter war zones, even to trade with neutrals. There is plenty of use for shipping in safer waters. The South American trade is already short of ships.

6. Keep American citizens out of war zones and out of the ships of belligerents. This is now being carried out.

Peace is not guaranteed by such a program. But at least we have done the most that can be done—short of embargoing all exports—to avoid entanglement. If we fight, it will be for emotional reasons—sympathy for the Allies, fear of future invasion, hatred of Hitler or his heirs and assigns.

It is going to be difficult, however, to choose an emotional cause with any stability. We shall feel one way if Germany is being beaten by the Allies, another way if the Allies are on the run, another way if Hitler is dropped overboard but Germany goes on winning, another way if Germany, Russia and Italy combine against the Allies, another way if Italy deserts Germany and joins the Allies, another if France splits off from England, another if Japan joins Russia and Germany, another if Japan joins England. There is no end to the moves on this chessboard.

The Treaty of Versailles is breaking up, just as every solemn European concert has broken up before it. The boundary lines are marching with the armies. Is it our duty to peg these boundaries? Can we peg them if we want to? Are they worth pegging? Or must they continue to shift in smoke and blood until a United States of Europe comes to banish them forever?

XII. AMERICA SOUTH

AFTER Waterloo, the affairs of Europe were dominated for a time by an axis composed of the kings of Russia, Austria and Prussia. It was called the Holy Alliance, and the man behind it was Prince Metternich of Austria. This holy outfit feared political democracy. Metternich felt about it as a Wall Street banker feels about communism. The French Revolution had scared the daylights out of sound, dynastic statesmen everywhere. It was high time that the common people be put back in the dog house, and kept there.

Here was this fellow Bolivar in South America. Following the lead of that other revolutionist, George Washington, he had made a successful rebellion and driven the armies of Spain into the sea. "Republics," no less, had been set up, with Constitutions patterned on the poisonous document to the north. Metternich proposed to send a military expedition to South America, and reconquer the erring colonies for the Spanish throne.

At this, Mr. George Canning, Foreign Secretary of England, became alarmed. He had designs on South America on behalf of *his* country. It was not territory he wanted, but open markets for English traders. So he proposed to President Monroe that the governments of England and the United States jointly guarantee the

South American republics, and thus warn off the Holy Alliance.

The President conferred with Jefferson, Adams and Madison about Canning's proposal. It was tempting. It showed that we were fast becoming a world power. But after much deliberation, Monroe decided to decline. He did not want to become entangled with any European nation. He decided to warn off the Holy Alliance single-handed. It took some courage to say to Austria, Prussia, Russia and Spain: "Gentlemen, keep out of the Western Hemisphere." He had, however, the tacit support of England. Thus the famous Monroe Doctrine was born. The year was 1823.

No law was passed, no order given. Congress took no formal action. President Monroe just made a speech. He said: "The American continents . . . are henceforth not to be considered as subjects for future colonization by any European power. . . . We should consider any attempt on their part to extend their system to any portion of this hemisphere as dangerous to our peace and safety." Such an attempt, he said, would constitute "an unfriendly act."

This is a mean term in the language of diplomacy. It is an upstage way of saying: "Try it, and we'll fight." The Holy Alliance understood and shied off. Russia shied out of Oregon at about the same time. Except for a few minor disputes and the tragic adventure of the Emperor Maximilian (an Austrian supported by a French army) in Mexico during our Civil War, European governments have continued to be gun-shy ever since.

There is no law, remember; it is just an administrative policy. When European statesmen have looked hungrily over-seas, American presidents since Monroe have dug his speech out of the files and said: "That goes for me, too."

Lately it is reported that a new holy alliance, also loathing political democracy, is looking hungrily at Latin America. The members are Germany, Italy and Japan. President Roosevelt has been reading over Monroe's speech again. Well?

As you know, there were European colonies in the Americas in 1823. England had Canada, the Bahamas, Jamaica, Trinidad and British Guiana. France had islands in the Caribbean and French Guiana. Holland had Curaçao and Dutch Guiana—once swapped for New York. Denmark had the Virgin Islands. Russia had Alaska and claims on Oregon. Spain still retained Cuba and Puerto Rico. Monroe made no objection to colonies already established. He put his foot down on military expeditions to get more. He recognized Bolivar's revolution as permanent.

Today the number of colonies has decreased. Alaska we bought from Russia, the Virgin Islands from Denmark. Puerto Rico we took from Spain in 1898 and at the same time made Cuba a separate nation under our protectorate.

A cartoonist recently represented Latin America as the belle of the ball, surrounded by suitors for her trade and affections—John Bull, Hitler, Mussolini, the Mikado and Uncle Sam. What does the belle think of these advances? To begin with, there is no such person. There are ten republics in South America, and ten in Central America and the Caribbean. Here they are, with their population, to refresh your memory. Quite an armful of belles.

South America		*Central America and Caribbean*	
Brazil	37,000,000	Mexico	16,500,000
Argentina	10,500,000	Cuba	4,000,000
Colombia	6,500,000	Haiti	3,000,000
Peru	5,500,000	Guatemala	2,400,000
Chile	4,000,000	El Salvador	1,600,000
Bolivia	3,500,000	Dominican Republic	1,500,000
Venezuela	3,000,000	Honduras	1,000,000
Uruguay	1,700,000	Nicaragua	750,000
Ecuador	1,500,000	Costa Rica	600,000
Paraguay	800,000	Panama	500,000

These twenty sovereign nations do not act as a unit, or two or three units. Bolivia and Paraguay have just terminated a bloody war in the Gran Chaco. Boundary disputes are frequent, and Carleton Beals anticipates an armed conflict between Brazil and Argentina. There have been a number of wars and many changes of frontiers since Bolivar marched down the Andes, and Father Hidalgo uttered the "cry from Dolores" which was to free Mexico from Spain. The nations vary in size from Brazil, with more square miles than the United States

1. Argentina
2. Chile
3. Bolivia
4. Paraguay
5. Uruguay
6. Brazil
7. Peru
8. Ecuador
9. Colombia
10. Venezuela
11. Panama
12. Costa Rica
13. Nicaragua
14. Honduras
15. Salvador
16. Guatemala
17. Mexico
18. Cuba
19. Haiti
20. Dominican Republic

(a large part of it steamy jungle, however) to Haiti, about as big as Vermont.

These countries resemble Europe in some respects. They have not achieved continental integration. Here are frontiers, standing armies, tariff walls, bitter rivalries, and old scores to settle. Here is Paraguay bottled up without a seaport. Here are serious minority problems. Citizens with the most Spanish or Portuguese blood tend to be on top; citizens with the most Indian or Negro blood at the bottom. But these minorities, unlike some of those in Europe, do not demand "self-determination." All twenty nations have lovely written constitutions, and most of them have virtual dictators in political command today. By and large since 1810, the intervals of genuine popular government have been few and far between. Mexico, Colombia, Chile and Costa Rica are said to be enjoying such an interval now, but there is no telling how long it will last.

We also find important differences from Europe. Latin America is fundamentally pioneer country. Plenty of arable land in most places prevents the acute population pressures of Europe. The nations remain largely in the late handicraft age, except for a few industrialized areas in Argentina, Chile, Brazil, Mexico. Their exports are primarily raw materials rather than factory products. This saves a lot of business competition and bad blood.

In all countries the Catholic Church is strong. Nearly all have the same official language—Spanish. Brazilians speak Portuguese, and Haitians speak French. All were once colonies of Spain or Portugal, and so have a common cultural pattern taken from the Iberian Peninsula. You have only to notice the way towns are arranged, with a central plaza and a stately church; you have only to see the rare courtesy shown to guests, hear the music of the guitar, to suspect that all these peoples have the same cultural mother. Underneath this pattern lies the older culture of the Indian, still strong in Mexico, Central America and Peru. There are cleavages in Latin America, but they are not so many, do not cut so deep, as those of Europe. The people would be stronger, and I think happier, if Bolivar had been able to forge a United States of South America. It may come.

What have we in common with our neighbors to the south? At first blush, it would seem that we have more in common with northern Europe than with them, and that they have more in common with Latin Europe than with us. This is undoubtedly true for many customs and traditions, as well as religion and language.

The bonds between the Americas are of a different sort. We are all New World people—pioneers. We all became independent of Old World masters—some of us gradually, like Brazil, others violently. We are all political democracies in theory, if not always in practice. All of us—even, I think, Canadians—want to stay out of Old World quarrels, and live our own lives in peace. We are practically a unit in being willing to fight military invasion from the Old World. We are bound together by our geographical isolation—even though Brazil is closer to Africa than to Florida.

We have much in common. But "gringos" are not greatly loved south of the Rio Grande. Many Americans have been—and are—intolerably superior and patronizing. Our business men form compact American colonies in Latin-American capitals, where many of them spend their idle hours drinking and sneering. We often hurt the feelings of our neighbors without realizing it. That word "American" is a case in point. Why should we pre-empt it to mean only citizens of the United States? Mexico, Santo Domingo, Lima, had great American universities when New England was still a roaring wilderness. There ought to be a one-word label for us—something like "Fords" or "Sams."

For a Latin American to look lovingly north is a little like a kitten nestling up to an Irish wolfhound. It may be all right, and it may not. Our government and business men have turned some pretty mean tricks in Latin America, first and last, and it will be long before they are forgotten. We bombarded Vera Cruz. Our marines overran Haiti until five years ago. But as Dr. Parker Moon points out, the United States government could have been far more imperialistic than it has been. We never tried to carve up South America the way the Great Powers carved Asia and Africa. The Monroe Doctrine worked both ways: It kept them out and it kept us out. We have established "spheres of influence," especially in the Caribbean, but have taken no outright colonies on the continent except the Canal Zone.

Latin Americans are of two minds about the Monroe Doctrine. It protects them, yes, but they have nothing to say about the terms of protection. It has undoubtedly been used to obtain commercial advantages for our business men. It is a one man show, not a club of political equals. For a time the southern countries went over bag and baggage to the League of Nations, hoping that this would furnish better protection. They are now disillusioned, as the League sinks into oblivion. We must never forget that if they grow too alarmed about the "Yankee peril," some of them may turn to Europe for protection against us. It is not likely, but neither is it impossible. We make a mistake if we think that Latin Americans are humbly grateful for the wolfhound. He can keep off other dogs. He can also eat kittens.

PENETRATION

What are the facts about the inroads of Old World traders in recent years? One hears much about the flood of Japanese goods. "Japanese merchants have quadrupled their exports to Latin America." This sounds alarming, and is true. But when you get down to cases, you find that the peak came in 1934, and that this all-time high represented *less than three per cent* of all Latin-American imports in that year. Japanese colonists are found all over South America, and on the whole they are welcome. Many make a meager living as fishermen, barbers, farmers. In Brazil they raise cotton, competing with the United States; also some silk, tea and rice, competing with Japan. The Japanese government, with China and Russia on its hands, and rich islands much closer to home, is not insane enough to be contemplating territorial conquests in Latin America.

Italy has been buying Argentinian wheat when the home crop was short. In 1937, Italy took 6 per cent of Argentina's exports, and supplied 5.5 per cent of her imports. No Latin-American country appears to do as much as 10 per cent of its foreign trade with Italy.

German trade figures are more impressive. The talented Dr. Schacht worked out an invention in international trade called the "Aski mark." German business men, via the German government, buy raw materials from Chilean business men, let us say. The materials are paid for in these Askis, or blocked marks. Chileans cannot swap this special money in the regular foreign exchange money market for dollars to buy Ford cars, or for pounds to buy English locomotives. *They can use them only to buy German goods.* This is not free trade. The system is expensive and inflexible. South Americans are not enamored of it, but it moves goods and is better than no sales at all.

In 1936, Germany supplied about 14 per cent of all imports to Latin America, representing 10.7 of Germany's export trade in that year. England sold about the same amount and the United States more than twice as much—29.4 per cent of all imports, to be exact. By monumental efforts, Germany raised its sales in 1937 and again in 1938. But sales from the United States also increased. They represented more than twice the share of any other country.

Since war began our exporters are accepting, more or less gracefully, a fine Christmas parcel of orders from Latin-American countries. The Germans cannot send them machinery at present, and whatever Aski marks remain unspent are useless now. The English also are unable to deliver much goods to South America while war continues. So Latin-American buyers must turn to the north, even for things which they prefer to buy from Europe. European airlines are folding their planes and resigning the field to the United States. In the last war we inherited almost half a billion dollars' worth of European business in South America, and lost it again when peace came. Financial editors are already advising exporters how to keep the business this time.

A difficulty has appeared already about means of payment. South American buyers have not much foreign exchange to contribute, and they have never liked the habit of some United States merchants of demanding cash in advance. Apparently the Latin countries can get handouts by the million dollars more easily than they can get ordinary short term credit from their Good Neighbor.

Nevertheless two weeks of war appears to have alienated them from their European suitors and turned their attention to this hemisphere more effectively than a year of diplomatic overtures by the United States, with the conference of Lima thrown in. One after another the Latin-American countries have declared neutrality in the present war and backed up the declaration with something more tangible. For instance, the Argentinians, who have the reputation of being Anglophiles, have formally protested against the English list of contraband articles, and actually quoted a Pan-American resolution to reprove Great Britain. They are burying old grudges against their neighbor Brazil and collaborating with her navy and that of Uruguay to patrol the coast and possibly the air against any activity by European submarines or European spies.

So the German political efforts of the last few years are not likely to be much more effective than the Aski marks as long as war goes on in Europe. There have been plenty of stories about these efforts. A huge amount of canned propaganda was sent over by that ineffable educator, Professor Doctor Goebbels. Some anti-semitism was stirred up. Nazi arms and money helped Dictator Vargas to power in Brazil. Once in power, he gave Nazi agents the gate.

Italian propaganda is said to have been strong in Peru, Chile, Uruguay and Paraguay. In Peru, school children have marched in black shirts, giving fascist salutes. Italian and German officers have been in various South American armies. General Franco's victory in Spain boosted the stock of Germany and Italy, and presumably a victory by the Nazis in Europe would boost it again.

Many individual cases can be found of political penetration by Germany and Italy. Listed one after another, they sound as if all Latin America were overrun. If we listed all our holdups in a week, one after another, it would sound as if the United States were composed solely of gunmen and their victims. This foreign propaganda should be watched with great care, and if possible, offset. But there are one hundred million people in Latin America, with plenty of ideas of their own.

It is clear that we cannot expect Latin Americans to rush into our arms as a defense against their European friends. They like certain European goods better than ours; they like many cultural contacts better; they like the training which European officers can give their armies. Their long experience, however, with aggressive thrusts from other continents, together with no small amount of political sagacity, indicates that they can take care of themselves and play a balance of power game. It would be very stupid of us to antagonize them further by ladling out the kind of good-will syrup which they have learned to distrust in the past.

A few neighborly acts will weigh more than millions of declarations. Noteworthy examples of such acts are the cancellation of the Platt amendment, modifying our protectorate over Cuba; the noble restraint with which the State Department has met the expropriation of American property in Mexico; some of the non-aggression treaties. Here are a few suggestions for further tangible acts:

1. Buy from Latin America as much as we can in preference to Old World countries. The studies in resources made earlier show that many raw materials now imported from abroad may be had, or may be developed, in this hemisphere. If we buy generously, we must export generously to foot the bill. High pressure selling methods should be discouraged.

2. Handle exports of munitions as a State Department task, and with extreme caution. Put the accent on naval equipment rather than on tanks and planes, which might be used in internal conflicts.

3. Encourage home production and self-sufficiency, even if it costs us some sales. We want these countries strong, not weak. Encourage rubber in Brazil, which helps to insure our supply in case of war abroad.

4. Invite Canadian delegates to any conferences on affairs of the hemisphere. This makes sense, and will please Latin-American statesmen besides.

5. Employ publicists at home rather than down there. North Americans need to know a lot more about their southern neighbors. Study and advertise the arts and cultural attainments of Latin America. Two expert horsemen from Chile, winning first honors at the New York Horse Show, did more to improve relations with their country than fifty sugary speeches by diplomats.

6. Sign more treaties for non-aggression and arbitration, with specific machinery for applying them. En-

courage the signing of such treaties among the southern nations themselves. Talk as little as possible about the Monroe Doctrine. Talk as little as possible about Pan-Americanism. Talk as little as possible about anything.

The Panama Conference on the current emergency will probably be over before these words are in print. If it turns out that Latin-American countries have shied away from a definite military alliance, their refusal may be ascribed to genuine neutrality. Some of their statesmen remember the pressure brought on them to follow the United States into the last war. Once burnt, twice careful. The United States will have to prove its own sober intention to stay at home in the Western Hemisphere before it will be a safe military partner for peaceful Latins. By the same token we have something to learn from our neighbors.

The Argentine-Brazilian coast patrol is a good sign and a good precedent. Another good sign is the suggestion by President Cardenas of Mexico for a continental navy for the Americas. Do we catch a hint here of a police force for the Western Hemisphere? It cannot be arranged hastily and does not need to be. No European nation is going to attack until turmoil subsides in Europe, which may not be for many years.

It cannot be too strongly emphasized that from the point of view of the ordinary citizen in Chile, Uruguay or Costa Rica, the United States is still just another big, dangerous Great Power—except that it is nearer and bigger. Until we live this down, Latin-American governments will enter Leagues and multilateral Monroe Doctrines, if at all, with their fingers crossed. Beneath their impeccable manners, their delegates will be asking: "What is the Big Bozo trying to put over this time?"

The situation abroad has furnished our neighbors with a strong warning against entanglements with European countries. Let it sink in without too much Yankee interpretation. Let us be reasonable about the war-time orders we are getting by default, and not expect them to exceed for very long the orders our importers send to Buenos Aires and Rio and the rest. Above all, let us be careful of mixing trade with politics. Heaven knows how many Americans at this moment advocate soaping down the southern peoples, offering to defend and succor them, simply because these gentlemen want more business.

The new western front is not a business proposition. It is not primarily a military proposition. It is a proposition in tolerance and understanding, prompted by an instinct for mutual survival in a storm-swept world.

XIII. HOME GUARD

IT is frequently said that if we do not help the Allies and if they lose the war, it will be our turn next. When Germany vanquishes the British navy we are done for.

It is true that if we help England to defeat Germany, we shall not be invaded. It is equally true that we shall not be invaded if we give no help—whatever the outcome of the European war, and whatever the fate of the British navy. We shall not be attacked in force by Germany, Italy, Russia, Japan, or anyone else. Why not? First, because we have nothing these nations want which cannot be obtained with far less difficulty nearer home—in the Balkans, Africa, Asia; and second, because our geographical position makes us invulnerable to successful invasion. No power or combination of powers, armed with any weapons now known or expected, can conquer the United States of America.

Even if our country lay within the borders of the Old World, dictators would pace the floors of their mountain retreats for a long, long time before deciding to attack. Since it lies in another hemisphere, over thousands of miles of ocean wastes, the project becomes fantastic.

If we want to fight to save the British Empire, that is one thing. Anglophiles can make out a case for it. But if we believe that we must rally to the defense of the Empire or be overrun ourselves, we have obviously never looked at a map, never examined the military difficulties of invasion, never trusted our own strength. Such talk is for old ladies and small boys in a panic.

Here is an estimate of the forces which would have to do the invading, together with our defense forces. The figures are taken from recent studies by Major George Fielding Eliot, and Major R. Ernest Dupuy.

Navy	*Battle-ships*	*Cruisers*	*Sub-marines*	*Destroy-ers, etc.*	*Total*
United States .	15	29	84	247	375
England	15	57	54	194	320
France	7	19	80	76	182
Germany	1	9	36	27	73
Italy	4	26	74	63	167
Japan	10	35	69	120	234
England and France	22	76	134	270	502
Germany and Italy	5	35	110	90	240
Germany, Italy and Japan ..	15	70	179	210	474

(Russia has a few submarines and gunboats, but no first-class capital ships.)

On the strength of these figures—not the total ships so much as the estimated fighting power—the American navy is almost a match for the English navy, is more than twice as powerful as the German and Italian navies combined, and could take on the navies of Germany, Italy and Japan without giving too much odds.

England and France together could completely smother Germany and Italy, and have heavy odds in their favor against Germany, Italy and Japan combined —22 battleships against 15. Battleships are the lads with the fire power.

The United States Navy Department released figures of warships appropriated for or under construction, for five of the great powers, as of November 15, 1938. They give us an idea of the building program, and serve to show that the same relative sea power is being maintained.

	Total tonnage	*Number of battleships*
United States	210,000	6
England	259,000	7
France	166,000	5
Germany	105,000	3
Italy	140,000	4

Japan refused to release figures, but naval authorities believe she is building three battleships of 40,000 tons each.

Now as to armies. I quote again from Eliot and Dupuy, for the year 1937.

	Regular army	*Trained reserves*	*Total*
United States	128,000	291,000	419,000
England	100,000	350,000	450,000
France	580,000	5,420,000	6,000,000
Germany	700,000	2,000,000	2,700,000
Italy	450,000	1,000,000	1,450,000
Japan	250,000	2,000,000	2,250,000
Russia	1,000,000	14,000,000	15,000,000
England and France .	680,000	5,770,000	6,450,000
Germany and Italy ..	1,150,000	3,000,000	4,150,000

The armies of the United States and England are small compared to those of the other powers. England banks on her navy; we bank on our geographical position. France, Germany, Italy and Russia have frontiers to guard in Europe, and feel that they need huge armies. The trained troops of France are more than twice as many as the trained troops of Germany. Why? Because Germany was allowed an army of only 100,000 by the Treaty of Versailles. The Treaty was not broken until after Hitler came in. Then a new army was constructed, but it takes time to build a great army, especially to train an adequate number of officers, of which the German army is still very short. France and England together are obviously a match for Germany and Italy. If the colossal army of Russia is added to either side, the balance tips. How good is the Russian army? Nobody knows—especially since the purges. Purges or no purges, it is probably stronger than the Czar's army.

How about comparative air forces? I have figures, but I will not give them. Airplanes can be built very rapidly —a month or two against four years for a battleship— and designs are constantly changing. The consensus of military opinion seems to be that the air forces of Germany and Italy outclassed those of England, France and Czechoslovakia in 1938, with Russia as usual an enigma. Not much value is given to Colonel Lindbergh's alleged report about Russia's lack of preparedness in the air. We have at least 2,000 fighting planes, and by next year may have twice as many, a fleet which will equal that of any nation except Germany and possibly Russia.

Majors Eliot and Dupuy believe that England and France would have an excellent chance of winning a war against Germany and Italy. They might lose many battles to begin with, but their superior resources would ultimately prevail. "The two Entente Powers possess vast financial and economic resources, drawn from their colonial empires and from other regions to which their superior sea power gives them access. There is no possible combination of naval power which can stand against the combined navies of the Entente in European waters." The French army, these experts say, is the best in Europe. Its title to pre-eminence rests upon its excellent officer corps, and its efficient staff and organization.

Air power may stop wars through fear of bombing,

but it cannot yet *win* wars once they are started. Men and resources must do that. The British Empire, as we noted earlier, and to a lesser extent the French Empire, have the resources.

The first job of Messrs. Hitler and Mussolini, before they come swarming over here, will be to lick England and France. Otherwise they would not dare release many ships or troops from Europe. This is going to be a tough assignment, if the Majors' figures are reliable. Even if they were victorious, the chances are that the people of Europe would be so exhausted that nobody would want to go swarming out on new conquests for a considerable period. It took Germany twenty years to recover from the last war. Politically, the invasion makes no sense at all.

HERE THEY COME!

Well, let us assume that England, France and Russia are somehow spirited out of the way. Hitler and Mussolini equip an Armada to conquer the United States, as Philip II equipped one to conquer England in the 1580's.

Here they come! A cloud of bombing planes precedes the main attack. Not so fast. . . . No plane yet built can cross from Europe to America with a load of bombs, let alone return. It can just about make it one way with a load of gasoline. The average bombing distance today is 600 miles from a good base, and return. Even Bermuda is beyond this range.

Here comes the combined navy anyway. Well, look at the damned thing: five battleships against our fifteen. If they use every ship they now have, and all they can build in the next ten years, we can still blow them into kingdom come. This isn't patriotic bragging, this is comparative fire power and muzzle velocity. We can blow to kingdom come any aircraft carriers they send, depriving them of a bombing raid by that method. (Incidentally, an aircraft carrier is not a good air base; it hasn't enough landing room.)

All right, let us see this through. Let us assume that our visible navy is somehow spirited out of the way. Now they can come roaring in! They cannot. They now have to meet our submarines and our air fleets, supported by excellent bases and the cream of mechanics and supplies, up and down the Atlantic coast. Can planes sink battleships? One did off the coast of Spain recently. They can certainly sink lesser craft as they sank the *Panay*, and what they would do to loaded troop-ships 3,000 miles from home is too painful to contemplate. We should have at least 4,000 planes in the air, and more coming off the assembly line every day.

Spirit away the submarines and planes. Now all they have to reckon with is coast defense guns and the army. Say 200,000 men are actually landed in Boston Harbor. Wait a minute. To transport and supply 200,000 troops requires 2,500,000 tons of merchant ships. Germany and Italy have not that many ships suitable for transatlantic traffic. So some of the troops will have to swim to Boston. Never mind; suppose somehow they get there.

Here are 200,000 Nazis and Fascists duly disembarked, marching up State Street. Out in Cambridge, Brookline, Newton, will be massed an American army of at least 400,000 trained soldiers, with millions of recruits drilling in the background, and spoiling for a fight. All our supplies, resources, transport facilities, will be mobilized by this time. The enemy can cut no vital arteries. We have a labyrinth of power lines, railroads, concrete highways, running in every direction, and three million square miles of territory to draw on. Lord, how we will run that landing force back into the sea!

First, meet and vanquish the armies and navies of England, France and their allies. Then, gentlemen, meet the American navy on its home front; then the American submarines and air force; then the American army, its tanks, its field artillery, and the massed might of an integrated continent.

Now let us turn to the other coast. Five thousand miles beyond San Francisco lies Japan. The Japanese military establishment has two considerable problems at present: China and Russia. If large forces are diverted to California, presently no Japanese may be left in China or Manchukuo. To attack the United States is the last thing the General Staff would dream of today, or for years to come.

But let us assume another political miracle. The fleet of Russian bombing planes at Vladivostok, the great

Russian army along the border, the armies of China, the guerilla hordes—all vanish and the full force of Japan's military machine is free for an attack upon the United States. The machine promptly encounters similar difficulties to those of Germany and Italy on the Atlantic coast—only more so. The ocean journey is almost doubled, leaving the invaders twice as far from their bases. In the old days, horsemen could go galloping around and live off the country, but modern armies, and especially navies, must have *bases* to which they can return when damaged, and from which they draw mountains of supplies. Japan has no base in the theatre of the Pacific, which our battleships and air forces would defend. We have them at Puget Sound, San Francisco, San Diego. We have one of the strongest fortresses on earth on the Hawaiian Islands. That fortress must be reduced before a Japanese naval force would dare proceed to our Pacific coast. It isn't healthy to have a great enemy fortress in one's rear. Even if our battle fleet were put out of commission, Hawaii could harbor enough submarines and airplanes to provide a terrible menace.

Our navy is half again as great as the Japanese navy. Once more we should be fighting from the *inside* of the war front, with all the resources of the continent at our backs, while the Japanese forces would be swinging wild, completely surrounded by the wastes of the Pacific, on the *outside* of the front. I apologize for wasting your time in this discussion. It would make an admirable topic for a debate in an insane asylum.

Suppose our foes came *simultaneously* on the Atlantic and Pacific. This would give us more trouble, but not much more. Our fleets can be shuttled from ocean to ocean through the Panama Canal. A lucky bomb from a suicide pilot might damage the Canal and prevent such strategic movement. One fleet, say our Atlantic squadron, would be beaten, and go limping back to port. What of it? The air fleets, the Atlantic submarines, the army, remain intact. New York or Charleston might be briefly bombarded, but no enemy would dare land an armed force, or could supply it if landed.

Let us try again. Suppose the foe landed in Canada, established bases, and marched down from there. Did you note what President Roosevelt said about defending Canada? What would our fleet be doing while any alien power landed in Canada? What would our submarines be doing to its supply ships? What would the British navy be doing? What would the Canadians themselves be doing?

A similar conclusion goes for Mexico, Central America, the Caribbean. North America can be, and should be, defended as a unit. When we were busy fighting the Civil War, the great powers sent the Emperor Maximilian over to conquer and rule Mexico. He was presently executed. Well, how about a German or Italian airplane base in South America, hidden in the jungle? How is it going to be built or supplied, without becoming visible to our bombers? If it is too small to disclose the supply train, we need not worry about it. Furthermore, none of our territory except the Canal Zone would be in its range.

PROGRAM FOR DEFENSE

Any way you look at it, the successful invasion of the United States is impossible with any weapons now known, provided we do not have to meet it with our bare hands. We already have a powerful navy, a good air force, an efficient army. How much larger should these forces be to give us complete insurance against attack? Let us follow Major Eliot again.

Build two more battleships for the Atlantic squadron, and perhaps a few fast pocket battleships. This is in addition to the present building program.

Enlarge the regular army to 240,000, the National Guard to 220,000, making 460,000 trained men altogether. Keep the army ready for immediate service.

Stimulate extensive research in all branches of aviation. Do not build great fleets of planes, but be ready to rush the latest design into mass production when an emergency arises. Designs are changing so rapidly that it is a waste to build 5,000 planes this year, only to replace them next year. Plans to build 12,000 war planes by 1940 are both hysterical and grossly inefficient.

Arm the Canal more strongly. Ring the Caribbean Sea, the "antechamber of the Canal," with naval and air bases. The base we now have at Guantanamo Bay in Cuba is the heart of the system, and should be greatly strengthened. It controls several passages into the Caribbean, as you can see from the accompanying map. Strengthen Key West, which is the gateway to the Gulf of Mexico. Put a new base at St. Thomas. Perhaps the British would give us two small islands—on account of war debts—one in the Bahamas, and one near Trinidad. These would make the defense circle even stronger.

On the Pacific, build a good base on the Aleutian Islands at Dutch Harbor, and, Ecuador permitting, one on the Galapagos Islands which lie off the Canal. These, with the Coast bases, and Hawaii as the spearhead, would keep us safe from any attack from the Pacific. *Make no attempt to defend the Philippines.* Any adventures by our armed forces into Japan's home waters are likely to meet with disaster. Our bases are too far away.

Embargo scrap steel and petroleum. Build up stock piles of essential raw materials—as suggested earlier.

Then we are about fixed. Let 'em come. But they will not dare to come. The only navy strong enough to give us real trouble is the British. We fought the British twice, why not again some day? Because, among other reasons, so long as Canada remains a part of the Empire, she serves as a hostage against attack.

The foundation of our defensive strategy is the navy. If an enemy comes he must be met well out to sea, far from our shores and firesides. If he comes, it must be with the strongest kind of naval support. As Major Eliot points out, one American destroyer could send to the bottom 10,000 fighting airplanes packed in the holds of a fleet of unconvoyed transports; one cruiser could

DEFENSE OF THE PANAMA CANAL. *From an article by Major George Fielding Eliot in the New Republic, March 30, 1938*

annihilate a million soldiers in such a fleet, with all their tanks, artillery and supplies.

The defense of any part of South America from foreign invasion is primarily a task for the navy and the air force. It should, of course, be a co-operative job. Argentina has a good navy, Brazil and Chile have modest ones. All South American countries have well-drilled armies, and man power. Our navy does not need to go down and sit in front of Rio or Buenos Aires. It can sit in the Caribbean, thus threatening the supply ships and the retreat of any naval force from Europe. The Caribbean region commands the wide bottleneck formed by the African and South American coasts.

I think it is perfectly safe to say that neither Germany, Italy nor Japan has military designs on South America at present. The home problems recited earlier will keep them away from both western continents. They can stir up local trouble, as we saw in the last Chapter, but it would be suicidal for them to despatch a large military establishment overseas at this particular point in history.

The good Lord and our ancestors have given us a well-nigh impregnable continent, and the cost of defending it against all comers is not great. But if we want to march away from that continent and make Japan safe for communism, Germany safe for minorities, or Tibet safe for mountain climbers, we shall have to treble, quadruple, our present armaments. In that event, all that I have said above will be in reverse. *We* shall be on the salt water outside, attacking navies with strong inside bases. *We* must see our great ships bombed by swarms of planes, torpedoed by submarines. *We* must gather the staggering tonnage of merchant vessels necessary to transport our young men abroad. *We* must meet the coast guns, the tanks, the well-organized defending armies on their home shores.

Furthermore, we must be prepared to surrender our political and economic liberties, bind our lives over to a dictatorial war government, to a vastly greater degree than would be the case in a purely defensive war. In the latter case, the navy would do most of the work. In the case of sending a great armament overseas, conscription must be resorted to, and millions of soldiers, with all their mechanized accouterment, must be provided for. At a guess, the cost of an aggressive war would be ten times that of a defensive war, let alone the cost of sacrificing nearly every vestige of the Bill of Rights.

Be calm, my fellow citizens. Neither Martians are coming, nor anyone else. Vote for adequate defense, but not one dollar, one soldier, one fourth-class gunboat for military adventures into the Old World. Our task, so far as one can scan the future today, is to hold the new western front.

XIV. HOW TO STOP DICTATORS

THE Nazis publish a newspaper called *Der Angriff*. One task of its editors is to prove to Germans that political democracy is an inferior form of government to the totalitarian state. Not long ago *Der Angriff* published a series of pictures showing American billboards with their cheery slogans: "There is no way like the American way"; "The world's highest wages," and so on. Just below, it ran a group of photographs taken in the United States, showing unemployed men at factory doors, slums, bums, breadlines, shacks of tenant farmers. It captioned the two exhibits: "Thank God, we have a better way."

In one sense, the Nazis have. There were six million unemployed in Germany when Hitler came into power. Today there are none. The outlook for German youth was black in 1933; now the future is dangerous but full of action. Factory chimneys were cold; now they are belching smoke. (Poetic image; German engineers save the smoke.)

We had better not try to win a contest against dictators simply by shouting about the blessings of "liberty" and "freedom." People do not eat liberty and freedom; these words make no jobs. For every cultivated American liberal who cares profoundly about the Bill of Rights, there are ninety-nine citizens in the lower income groups who care more profoundly about employment and security. Americans have political democracy rooted deep in their folklore, but it is rash to suppose that they are prepared to defend it at the price of permanent economic misery. If we value our liberties of speech, press and ballot, we shall have to make the economic machine work better than it has worked since October, 1929. With twenty million Americans on relief, those cheery posters warrant a razzing from Hitler or anybody else.

Why were Italians converted to fascism? Because they were suffering from bad economic conditions, unemployment, fear of communism, and were disappointed over Italy's share in the spoils of the Versailles Treaty. They turned to a Strong Man.

Why were Germans converted to Naziism? Millions of them, remember, had been voting a socialist ticket. They were suffering from unemployment, terrible economic conditions, poor food, savage reparation payments, unending debts to foreigners, the iron ring of Versailles, the middle-class fear of communism. They turned to a Strong Man.

Why do the people of many nations in Europe support dictators, and hang out a "To Rent" sign on their houses of parliament? Because of desperate economic conditions, unemployment, insecurity. Will such conditions produce a Strong Man in France, in England, some day? If they continue long enough, they probably will. There are already signs of it in Paris. They once produced a Napoleon in France, following a Queen who said: "Let them eat cake."

When will the people of the United States turn to a Strong Man? When they are fed up with being half fed. Yet when President Roosevelt proposes to do something about the one-third of the nation which is underfed, thousands of well-fed Americans roar with rage, and accuse him of inspiring class hatred, and destroying the nation by paternalism. Still more ironically, they accuse him of trying to become a dictator. So you see, it isn't easy to meet the challenge of the real dictators, in a real political democracy, where citizens have the constitutional right to raise bitter objections to government action.

How do European dictators get rid of unemployment? They get rid of it chiefly by putting citizens to work in armament factories and in labor camps devoted to building fortifications. They also put a lot of them directly into the army. Where do they get the money? The government commandeers available savings by forced loans. It also "creates" more money by printing bonds. It makes the banks take the bonds, and then draws checks to the amount of the bonds. These savings and "new" money are turned over to the munition workers and other government employees, who spend them in the stores on pay day. This gives business activity to storekeepers, wholesalers, manufacturers, farmers. Things look prosperous. Unemployment is greatly reduced.

Instead of capital being invested in the expansion of private industry as in the past, it is now expended in government industry—most of it to construct such fine, productive assets as tanks, bombers and battleships. *But the temporary effect is just as stimulating.* The trouble is that government debts are piling up, with no productive resources out of which to pay them.

In this country we have also been piling up public debts in default of the expansion of private enterprise. The reason for this we cannot go into here; enough to say that the expansion rate of private enterprise has been dropping with foreign trade, with the population curve, with the end of new pioneer country to develop. It won't come up in a hurry. But most of the proceeds of our public loans have gone into better things than shot and shell. They have gone to help farmers, help home owners, to build highways and schools, to save good American soil against erosion. Some outlays have been wasted, but not from the point of view of managers of grocery stores, on Saturday nights.

As we noted in the last Chapter, we must now pile up some debts—or tax more heavily—for strengthening our military and naval defenses. Major Eliot has demonstrated that it will not necessarily amount to a great sum. This will stimulate business here as it has in Europe, where some fifteen billions were spent for armaments in 1938. But we must never forget that to spend *more* for armaments than is essential for defense, is a criminal waste, when so much important construction is waiting to be done on the peacetime front. Yet business men raise practically no objections about a budget unbalanced by submarines, and raise merry hell about one unbalanced by school buildings.

Our chief economic task today is to find a way to stimulate business activity and reduce unemployment, without piling up debts which may ultimately be repudiated. We have already seen twenty billions of foreign loans repudiated. We have already seen how forlorn is the hope of solving the problem by increasing our exports. The overwhelming proportion of our business is done in the home market. Seventy-one per cent of our families earn less than $2,500 a year; forty-two per cent have incomes below the standard of health and decency. These people could consume much if not all of our surplus production, and as I have pointed out earlier, any "dumping" we do should be in their direction.

I believe, however, that we can eventually supply them and even increase production without resorting to further subsidies. Engineers calculate that we could produce half again as much as we do now.[1] The factors favorable for a well-oiled economic machine are all present to a degree unknown in European countries: plenty of resources, technical skill, productive capacity, man power, and a huge market eager for goods in the lower income groups.

[1] See the *Chart of Plenty*, by Harold Loeb; also the report of the National Survey of Potential Product Capacity.

INVENTIONS WANTED

Foreign and domestic affairs are closely interwoven. This can readily be admitted without accepting the implied corollary that we have to look abroad for the solution of home problems. The Nazis are ahead of us in finding jobs for unemployed men, and in certain financial inventions. We answer this by looking down our noses and saying that the inventions are "unsound," and therefore unworkable. The Nazis answer that they are working; and they are.

Dr. Schacht was nobody's fool in the field of finance. His Aski marks worked well enough to frighten Wall Street and the City of London. His inventions for finding the money to rearm Germany worked well enough to frighten the world into imitation—not only from fear of attack, but to help lift the curse of unemployment. In 1932, the League of Nations estimated world unemployment at more than thirty millions. From that peak it has declined as armaments have gained.

For all the superiority of the United States in many departments, we might take a similar road unless we seriously tackle this fundamental problem. We haven't yet. Many of us still think that a ten year depression is only a temporary upset, and things will right themselves as soon as the government stops interfering, and confidence is restored. If it were only so simple! Things will not right themselves even if every government official is kicked clean out to sea beyond Bermuda. Will "confidence" reverse the birth rate, open up more free land? There was plenty of confidence in 1929, but in that year, according to the Brookings Institution, two thirds of our national savings failed to find an outlet in productive investment.

These stony facts must be admitted by enough Americans so that new financial experiments may be given a reasonable trial. We have all the material requisites for an ample livelihood, but what good has that done a Louisiana sharecropper? So little good that he fell on his knees before a Huey Long.

Our material superiority, our splendid geographical isolation, give us the clear responsibility to take first place in finding a solution to unemployment and insecurity. It must be a solution sounder than activity generated by rotten war debts, foreign loans, Aski marks, raids on Ethiopians, and towering armaments. Is prosperity to be eternally nourished on bad debts?

If we can't find the solution, who can? Is the country of Eli Whitney, Steinmetz and Edison to bow to Dr. Schacht? Are all the inventors dead? We must recognize that developing a financial invention is similar to designing any other engine, and that too many obstacles must not be placed in the path of trying it out.

Only people talking in their sleep call the Nazis conservative and capitalistic. They are very radical. They have started a revolution from which any prudent capitalist should run for his life. Some of their measures may be as crazy as the Townsend Plan, and far more harsh, but others are efforts more disciplined and serious than any we have undertaken to make the economic machine go round.

There is a Nazi menace to us, and this is it. It does not lie in the direction of arms, airplane bases, Bunds, or even petty Fuehrers in Jersey City or California. It lies in the indisputable fact that they have found a kind of answer to the hardest problem an adult civilization has ever faced. There is almost no unemployment in Germany, Italy, or Russia.

Unity. The United States. We are integrated in land and resources. We have to become integrated and unified in facing this grave and difficult task. If we can find an invention, or a series of inventions, to conquer unemployment without piling up a mountain of debt, some day to be repudiated, we shall be as immune to foreign isms and ideologies as an iron dog is to rabies. By the same token, our example will strike home to the people of other countries, uneasy under their Strong Men, yet not knowing where else to turn.

In simplest terms, the inventors must find a method which will permit Americans to buy back what they can make. Such a method would keep everybody employed. Millions of them cannot do so now because of jams in the price structure, in the debt structure, in the distribution of income, in the flow of savings into new investment. Like Alice in Wonderland, they can just stand and look at the beautiful garden without being able to get into it.

We need an invention that will neutralize, scale down, transform, the present debt burden, and prevent it from accumulating in the future—an invention that will lead steadily to a pay-as-you-go economy. A rapidly expanding industrial system can tolerate compounding debt. It did in America from 1830 to 1930. A non-expanding, or slowly expanding system, cannot tolerate it. Business men often express horror at an unbalanced federal budget. They apparently forget that private enterprise as a whole has never balanced its budget, has never been on a pay-as-you-go basis. Net private debt—mostly corporate—has grown from some forty billions in 1910 to almost two hundred billions today. By comparison the present federal debt of forty billions is mere chickenfeed. The 1922-1929 Boom was reared on private debt, just as the 1933-1937 Recovery was reared on public debt.

We need inventions that will finance a growth in *intensive* capital outlays, which raise living standards of a stationary population. *Extensive* capital outlays for a rapidly growing population are no longer feasible. We need a workable invention to convert bonds into stocks with reasonable justice to all concerned. A stock is seldom paid off as to principal, and carries no fixed interest charge; dividends are disbursed only if earned. Such an invention is urgently needed at this very moment for the railroads. We could use an invention for financing public works, federal, state and local, on a giant revolving fund basis, without interest charges.

We need inventions for melting out the rigidities of administered or monopoly prices. We need inventions for redistributing the national income, through taxation or otherwise, so that more of it will be spent and less of it saved to rot in reserves. Hoarding is one thing that the modern money network cannot tolerate without disaster. We need inventions for improved methods of handling social security funds, crop controls, collective bargaining. As sensible a general program as I have seen recently is that announced by a group of economists from Harvard and Tufts, called *An Economic Program for American Democracy*, and published by the Vanguard Press.

Such a program is as much a part of the national defense as wind tunnels for airplane experiments, or the naval base at Guantanamo.

xv. HERE WE ARE

HERE we are, one hundred and thirty millions of us, in the grandest slice of continent on earth. We have right under our feet almost everything we need to give the last family a decent standard of living. We do not need to go out and take anything, because we have it here. We do not need to fight anybody unless they come and try to take away what we have. God help them if they do.

Our country lies wholly in the temperate zone, in the latitudes where men can work harder and think straighter than in hotter or colder climates. We have a great interlocked coal and iron industry, and beyond it prodigious grain and grazing lands, and a mammoth central river basin with easy grades for transport. Half the world's energy is generated within our borders. Ninety-eight per cent of it comes from oil, coal and falling water; only two per cent from man and animal.

We have no territorial ambitions, no surplus population to be exported, like Japan's; no driving need for a place in the sun. The protection of citizens and investments abroad is less closely identified with the national honor than it was in 1900. Dollar Diplomacy has been succeeded by the good neighbor policy. The marines are out of Nicaragua, Haiti and Santo Domingo. Twenty billions in foreign debt, gone beyond recall, have made most of us apathetic about the glories and benefits of loaning money around the world. Ninety-five per cent of our business is in the home market, and always has been, except for a tumorous growth in the war years.

We cannot be good neighbors by joining economic wars for export trade, when we do not really need the trade. If exports are to be subsidized, if there is dumping to be done, let us dump at home. Good neighbors exchange food with one another when the milkman doesn't appear, or the icebox breaks down. They don't try to sell the parlor furniture and the family silver to the people across the street.

We have no yearnings for military achievement, no traditional enemies, no *revanche* to appease. Our only ancient enemy is England, and Canada is a bond so close between us that it is quite incredible that we should ever fight again. We do not need to go totalitarian. We do not need flags, swastikas, Klieg lights, goose-steppers at the salute, military mobilization, to show the world how strong we are. The world knows how strong we are. Candidates for public office engage in bitter struggles with their rivals, but when the vote is counted, the loser sends the winner a telegram of congratulation.

We are steeped in the habits of political democracy. We have practiced it for one hundred and fifty years without serious interruption, except in 1861 and 1917. We have no parties trying to restore the monarchy, as in France; no pretenders plotting for a throne; no shirted rabble drilling and shouting for a strong man to save us. We have no domination by a state church. We have no official snoopers censoring our news, telling us what to think. We are not full of grandiose notions about our "Roman" tradition, our "Aryan" tradition, our "Celtic" blood. The melting pot took care of that.

We have no festering minorities waiting to cry "self-determination," and set up sovereign states. We have no vested aristocracy sneering at peasants and city scum. We have no fixed classes, into which one is born for life. Telephone girls talk back to tycoons. Men working on the highways do not touch their hats to anybody. Sand hogs, high tension men, structural steel workers, locomotive engineers, can look at Wall Street bankers and tell them to go to hell. And do. We lack a strongly class-conscious proletariat. As mechanical power increasingly displaces human muscle, it begins to seem improbable that we ever shall get one. First, free lands in the West, then batteries of humming turbines, have enabled us largely to bypass that phase of history.

Most of us have already learned that mass production demands an equivalent in mass consumption, and that the stocks and bonds of the rich are so much wallpaper unless those not so rich have money to buy motors, gasoline, refrigerators, radios, electric power, bathtubs, safety razors, silk stockings, and the other goods the mass production industries stand ready to produce. But we still have to find a practicable financial invention to get adequate purchasing power passed around.

Washington is the most important city on earth today. It is the symbol of an integrated continent, without a tariff barrier, a language difference, an armed frontier, an alien cultural pattern, from Atlantic to Pacific. Our neighbor to the north is a brother of the same pioneer family; our neighbor across the Rio Grande is at least nearer to political democracy, as we know it, than any other Latin-American country today. Diaz is dead.

We can afford to do what no other nation can afford to do. We have no national interest outside the Western Hemisphere so vital that if it is threatened we must fight. We can remain neutral in any Old World quarrel if we desire it. We know that we can defend ourselves, probably even our entire hemisphere, from any power, almost any combination of powers. By the same token we know that to launch our armies abroad can only be accomplished at a fabulous cost, with no certainty of achieving what we set out to do.

If we fight it will not be to serve the national interest but because our emotions are aroused—fear, hate, pity. We have no enemy to fear. It is monstrous to kill carpenters and farmers because we hate their leaders, whom our guns cannot reach. Our pity and sympathy should go to all the tortured people of Europe, trapped in a world they never made.

Let us watch our emotions as never before. Let us beware of ideological crusades to march out and make the world safe for something, such as liberty or democracy, or *against* something, such as aggression or the rule of force. We cannot force liberty down the throats of another people. Trying to, we lose our own. We cannot halt aggression by ourselves becoming an aggressor. We cannot check the rule of force by force. These fighting words and slogans are full of madness, a lesson which Versailles should have taught us. We can help somebody to hammer somebody to a bloody pulp, but this action is not dignified by giving it a lofty name.

Our destiny lies here in the West. This is our land, our home. Fortunate above all others, stronger than any other, in a sense we have civilization in our keeping. The responsibility is passing from the Old World to the new. We may not be worthy of it, but we are getting it by default. While Europe destroys, we can build. While universities and laboratories crash beneath the bombs, we can build new universities and laboratories. If the ruin spreads, we may indeed become the surviving outpost of human culture on this planet.

If we are only going to play power politics with the rest of the world, we do not deserve this trust. And if we fight, we shall throw away not only our chance to lead the world, but the best of the civilization we now possess. We have a watch to keep on the western front, a solemn obligation to maintain a strong citadel of democracy, of hope, in a world stumbling into darkness.

APPENDIX

Explanation of Methods Used in Preparing Tables 1, 2 and 3

Tables 1 and 2

Estimates of raw material supplies can be found in a number of publications. For instance, Brooks Emeny in *The Strategy of Raw Materials*, Macmillan, 1936, gives a chart for 22 materials and 7 countries. A report written by John C. deWilde for the Foreign Policy Association, September 1936, gives a table for 36 materials, 13 countries and their dependencies. Erich Zimmermann in his great study, *World Resources and Industries*, Harper, 1933, gives many useful tables and diagrams.

I have studied these and other sources and have used them as a check on the accompanying tables which, however, have been freshly compiled.

Most of the percentages shown are calculated from the *Statistical Yearbook* for 1937-38 of the League of Nations. The few items given in dollars come from Leo Hausleiter, *The Machine Unchained*, Appleton-Century, 1933. The acreage of arable land comes from O. W. Willcox, *Nations Can Live at Home*, Norton, 1935, and the railroad mileages from the *World Almanac*. Other items are taken from the *Minerals Yearbook* for 1938 of the U. S. Bureau of Mines, and from private sources.

To allow for seasonal fluctuations in wheat and corn crops, and to avoid the effect of recent crop reductions, average production for the years 1930-34 was used. In other commodities, however, notably certain minerals, the picture is changing so fast that an average of years would mask some important trends. Here the latest year was used for which complete figures are available, in most cases 1936, in mercury and silk 1935, in sugar and cotton 1937-38, in coal, oil, steel, pig iron, potash, nickel and automobiles, 1937.

Allowance of a few points plus or minus should be made for occasional estimates and approximations in the sources themselves, and for fluctuations in production from year to year. With this reservation, I think the proportions given are as accurate as can be obtained anywhere. So far as I know, no other compilation exists which makes the comparisons shown here.

Table 3

The figures in the two preceding tables were used in preparing this qualitative exhibit. In addition, the production of other countries in the Western Hemisphere was of course considered, and allowances were made so far as possible for consumption requirements and existing natural reserves. No statement of this kind can be exact. Figures would have made little sense. But whether a country has plenty of coal, a deficiency of coal, or no coal discovered at all, can be stated, and useful conclusions drawn about resource strength. It must also be remembered that as technology changes, resource strength or weakness may become a different story within a few years.

SELECTED BIBLIOGRAPHY

Armstrong, Hamilton Fish, *We or They*, Macmillan, 1938

Beals, Carleton, *The Coming Struggle for Latin America*, Lippincott, 1938

Beard, Charles A., *The Idea of National Interest*, Macmillan, 1934

—— *The Open Door at Home*, Macmillan, 1934

Chambers, Frank P., *The War Behind the War*, Harcourt, 1939

Cless, G. H., Jr., *The Eleventh Commandment*, Macmillan, 1938

Crowther, Samuel, *America Self-Contained*, Doubleday, Doran, 1933

Dean, Vera Micheles, *Europe in Retreat*, Knopf, 1939

Eliot, George Fielding, *Bombs Bursting in Air*, Reynal & Hitchcock, 1939

—— *The Ramparts We Watch*, Reynal & Hitchcock, 1938

Eliot and Dupuy, *If War Comes*, Macmillan, 1937

Emeny, Brooks, *The Strategy of Raw Materials*, Macmillan, 1934

Foreign Policy Association, New York. Various publications

Frank, Jerome, *Save America First*, Harper, 1938

Gould, Kenneth, *Windows on the World*, Stackpole, 1938

Griswold, A. Whitney, *The Far Eastern Policy of the United States*, Harcourt, 1938

Gunther, John, *Inside Europe*, Harper, 1938

Hacker and Modley, *The United States, A Graphic History*, Modern Age, 1937

Hausleiter, Leo, *The Machine Unchained*, Appleton-Century, 1933

Herring, Hubert, *And So to War*, Yale University Press, 1938

Horrabin, J. F., *An Atlas of Current Affairs*, Knopf, 1934

Hutton, Graham, *Survey after Munich*, Little Brown, 1939

League of Nations, *Statistical Yearbook*, Geneva, 1938

Millis, Walter, *The Road to War*, Houghton Mifflin, 1935

Moon, Parker T., *Imperialism and World Politics*, Macmillan, 1926

Plan Age, Vol. III, No. 9: "The Maintenance of American Neutrality," Washington, December, 1937

Raushenbush, Stephen and Joan, *The Final Choice*, John Day, 1937

Smith, J. Russell, *Men and Resources*, Harcourt, 1937

U. S. Department of Commerce, *Economic Review of Foreign Countries*, 1937

U. S. Department of the Interior, *Minerals Yearbook*, 1938

Willcox, O. W., *Nations Can Live at Home*, Norton, 1935

Zimmerman, E. W., *World Resources and Industries*, Harper, 1936

INDEX